DON'T TELL US IT CAN'T BE DONE!

ALTERNATIVE CLASSROOMS IN CANADA AND ABROAD

EDITED BY CHUCK CHAMBERLIN

Canadian Cataloguing in Publication Data

Main entry under title:

Don't Tell Us It Can't Be Done! : alternative classrooms at work in
    Canada and abroad

(Our schools/our selves monograph series ; no. 15)
Includes bibliographical references.
ISBN   0–921908–18–0

1. Non-formal education.   2. Free schools.
I. Chamberlin, Charles R., 1935–.   II. Our Schools/Our Selves Education
Foundation.   III. Series.

LC45.3.D76 1994   371'.04   C94–930989–3

This book is published by Our Schools/Our Selves Education Foundation,
107 Earl Grey Road, Toronto, Ontario, M4J 3L6.

For subscribers to *Our Schools/Our Selves: a magazine for Canadian
education activists*, this is issue #34, the fourth issue of volume 5.

The subscription series Our Schools/Our Selves (ISSN 0840-7339) is
published 6 times a year. Publication Mail Registration Number 8010.
Mailed at Centre Ville, Montréal, Québec.

Design and typesetting: Tobin MacIntosh.

Cover design: Vidal Alcolea.

Cover photo: Point Blank School; photo by John Phillips.

Our Schools/Our Selves production: Keren Brathwaite, Loren Lind, Doug
Little, Bob Luker, Tobin MacIntosh, Nick Marchese (Co-ordinating Editor),
George Martell (Executive Editor), Satu Repo, Harry Smaller.

Printed in Canada by La maîtresse d'école inc., Montréal, Québec.
Copyright © Our School/Our Selves Education Foundation
April, 1994

Acknowledgements

This book was made possible by support from the University of Alberta during a study leave.

Additional support was provided by Felix Ormaetxea and Grupo Educativo Hezibide in Mondragon, Spain; by Hanna Poulson and the Tvind Schools in Denmark; and by Karl-Georg Ahlström and Uppsala University in Sweden.

The willing efforts of chapter authors have added breadth to the work, and for that I am indebted to Bill Lee, Rick Moore, Don Taylor, Karl-Georg Ahlström, Merle Kennedy, Christina Gustaffson and Karen Day.

The critical reading of the chapters by students in my Reflective Teaching class was invaluable in revising an early draft.

To each of these, my great thanks for their support and contributions.

Chuck Chamberlin
Edmonton, Alberta
March, 1994

Contents

Dedication

This book is dedicated to my wife, Linnie, whose love has made all the difference in what has been possible for me to do these last six years.

Introduction

Life In Schools
Chuck Chamberlin

Schools differ. *Schooling* is everywhere very much the same.

John Goodlad
A Place Called School (1984)

Goodlad's point is that regardless of apparent external differences among schools, the essence of the schooling experience for children is much the same everywhere. Nor was Goodlad generalizing from vague impressions. He and a corps of researchers had just completed an exhaustive study of 1,350 teachers and their 17,163 students and 8,624 parents in 38 diverse schools in the United States. Detailed observations in over 1,000 classrooms were supplemented with extensive interviews and questionnaires to provide Goodlad with one of the most comprehensive descriptions of classroom life available. And, while the schools differed in location (urban, suburban, rural), size, characteristics of student population, family incomes, and many other ways, Goodlad confidently concluded that the *sameness* of schooling was impressive.

In describing life in classrooms, Goodlad lists nine "patterns of teaching and learning" which were surprisingly pervasive in the 13 elementary schools, 12 junior highs and 12 senior highs. First was the dominance of whole-class teaching. Although there were examples of small group and individualized learning, teaching normally was to the whole group, "conditioned by the need to maintain orderly relationships" (p. 123).

Second, within these whole-group activities "each student essentially works and achieves alone" rather than in "shared, collaborative" ways (p. 123). Competitiveness among individual children was the common finding.

Third, the teacher was the "central figure" in determining classroom activities, with virtual autonomy to decide on materials used, classroom organization, instructional procedures, and the general tone of classroom life. Consequently, students made "scarcely any decisions about their learning.... Nearly 100% of the elementary classes were almost entirely teacher dominated with respect to seating, grouping, content, use of space, time utilization, and learning activities" (p. 229) as were 90% of the junior high and 80% of senior high classes.

Fourth, "the domination of the teacher is obvious in the conduct of instruction...in either frontal teaching, monitoring students' seatwork, or conducting quizzes" (pp. 123-4). Seldom did students learn from one another, and even when students did work in small groups, they usually did the same teacher-determined tasks. About 70% of instruction was talk, 75% by teachers. The bulk of this teacher talk was telling, and less than 1% "required some kind of open response involving reasoning or perhaps an opinion from students" (p. 229). Student talk was usually to give an informational answer to the teacher's question.

Fifth, "there is a paucity of praise and correction of students' performance ... (or) guidance on how to do better next time" (p. 124).

Sixth, there was very little variety in the types of classroom activities teachers used. Mostly, children listened to teachers, wrote answers to questions, and took tests. These dominant activities "transcend teachers, grade levels, and subjects" (p. 124), while A-V aids, field trips, guest lecturers, drama, role play, dance, and hands-on manipulation of materials "are rarely used as accompaniments or alternatives to textbooks and workbooks as media of instruction" (p. 124). The textbook often was nearly the sole source of knowledge, while the workbook provided the follow-up activities for students to do. Goodlad describes the common classroom pattern as follows:

> ... the teacher explaining or lecturing to the total class or a single student, occasionally asking questions requiring factual answers; the teacher, when not lecturing, observing or monitoring students working individually at their desks; students listening or appearing to listen to their teacher and occasionally responding to the teacher's questions; students working individually at their desks on reading or writing assignments; and all with little emotion, from interpersonal warmth to expressions of hostility. (p. 230)

One consequence of these dominant teaching patterns is that, "One learns passivity. Students in schools are socialized into it virtually from the beginning" (p. 233). Good students have quickly learned that teachers are active, dominate the talking, make nearly all the decisions, and expect students to accept their passivity unquestioningly and without resistance.

Goodlad notes that the common pattern of "the bland repetitive procedures of lecturing, questioning, monitoring, and quizzing now characterizing classrooms" (p. 249) seems dulling:

> And one wonders about the meaningfulness of whatever is acquired by students who sit listening or performing relatively repetitive exercises, year after year. Part of the brain, known as Magoun's brain, is stimulated by novelty. It appears to me that students spending twelve years in the schools we studied would be unlikely to experience much novelty. Does part of the brain just sleep, then? (p. 231)

Further, Goodlad felt boredom resulted from "the flat, neutral emotional ambiance.... Boredom is a disease of epidemic proportions" (p. 242) leading students to doze or withdraw into private fantasy when teacher telling began, or, outside school, to turn to TV, alcohol and drugs to provide a temporary escape.

Seventh, variety of teaching techniques was greatest in the lower grades, but from the upper elementary grades on the patterns described above were "quite commonly descriptive" (p. 124).

Eighth, many students were passively content with classroom life. Generally, they had been so socialized into these

3

patterns of classroom living that they were accepted as normal. This despite the ninth pattern, that students often did not understand nor have time to finish what their teacher wanted them to do.

Goodlad sees a steady decline from lower to upper grades in teachers' support of students as persons and learners. Classrooms become more routinized in instructional practices, as teachers focus more on the curriculum and the textbook and less on the child. The consequence is that schooling plays a minimal role in the humanization of knowledge, with students seeing little relevance of the textbook knowledge learned for tests. Not surprisingly, "Teachers and classes appeared to occupy positions of declining significance in the lives of the young" (p. 126).

Similarly, the classroom setting became decreasingly attractive as observers moved from lower to upper grades. Classes in the lower grades "generally were rich in displays of children's art products, as well as posters, plants, and other decorative features.... The picture is of increasing drabness as one moves upward through the grades" (pp. 227-8). Goodlad asks, "Why should the workplace of teachers, children, and youth be so sterile, and why do those in this workplace do so little about its aesthetic qualities?" (p. 227).

The goals normally achieved in these classrooms were in lower intellectual processes, with "repetitive attention to basic facts and skills" (p. 236). Schools did not appear to be promoting intellectual development:

> ... the ability to think rationally, the ability to use, evaluate and accumulate knowledge, a desire for further learning. Only rarely did we find evidence to suggest instruction likely to go much beyond mere possession of information to a level of understanding its implications and either applying it or exploring its possible applications. (p. 236)

This seemed partly to result from teachers being oriented to teach particular things — as they were taught in school. Relating these particular things to some larger purpose for schooling is not something teachers think about very much or have been prepared to do, Goodlad believes.

Goodlad notes that school goals are particularly idealistic in the social, civic, cultural and personal domains where altruistic expectations for understanding others with different value systems, constructive self-criticism, satisfying relations with others, and creative expression are emphasized. Yet,

> I conclude that the schools in our sample were contributing minimally to such goals. With respect to some, they were rather neutral. With respect to others, they contributed negatively. (p. 239)

The hidden curriculum embedded in the roles and relationships Goodlad observed reveals "a great hypocrisy" between goals of individual flexibility, originality, and creativity, and what children really learn.

> From the beginning, students experience school and classroom environments that condition them in precisely opposite behaviors — seeking "right" answers, conforming, and reproducing the known. (p. 241)

Teachers believe this socialization process is essential to the conduct of schooling. It is very deliberate in the primary grades, and is fully established and rarely questioned after the upper elementary grades.

> The dominant role of the teacher, limited opportunity for student-initiated activity, and quiet passivity of the class group, become virtues to be reinforced. Deviation may be tolerated, but it is neither condoned nor rewarded. Usually the socialization process, as powerful among teachers as among students, simply discourages or ultimately suppresses deviation. (p. 266)

Further, the organization of schools into grade levels, each with its chunk of each subject, carries with it a similar set of mandates.

> The age-grade division encourages a short-term view of what is to be learned — topics and facts rather than basic concepts and relationships; focus on what can be acquired in a week or semester and then measured rather than the long-time maturation of intellectual capabilities; observing rules rather than becoming increasingly self-disciplined. The division into subjects and periods encourages a segmented rather than an inte-

grated view of knowledge. Consequently, what students are asked to relate to in schooling becomes increasingly artificial, cut off from the human experiences subject matter is supposed to reflect. (p. 266)

The portrait Goodlad paints of schooling is one of textbook and workbook based whole-class instruction, with teacher-directed recitation and lecture, followed by quizzes and exams. Nearly all the decisions are made by teachers, and students learn to be passive, give the right answers, and follow the rules set out by the teacher and school. Conformity is rewarded, both for students and teachers. The effects of 12 or 13 years of such patterns stultify the intellect and children's creativity, ignore goals of social, civic, ethical and cultural growth, reward competitiveness while punishing cooperation as cheating, and dehumanize both children and teachers, Goodlad concludes.

Worse, "Over the years, these ways of schooling have proved to be extraordinarily resistant to change" (p. 267), he contends. Though we have moved from desks screwed to the floor to movable tables and chairs, whole-class, teacher-directed activities continue to dominate.

This view of schooling as resistant to change is the theme of another study by Larry Cuban, titled *How Teachers Taught* (1984). Cuban studied records of classroom practices in the period 1890-1980. He was interested in the extent to which school reform efforts changed teaching practices and children's school experience, as well as why innovations succeeded or failed. He focused on the teacher-centered/child-centered continuum for his research, and defined them as follows. Teacher-centered instruction indicators are:

- Teacher talk exceeds student talk during instruction.
- Instruction occurs frequently with the whole class; small group or individual instruction occurs less frequently.
- Use of class time is determined by the teacher.
- The classroom is usually arranged into rows of desks or chairs facing a blackboard with a teacher's desk nearby. (p. 3)

Student-centered instruction contrasts sharply in these ways:

- Student talk on learning tasks is at least equal to, if not greater than, teacher talk.

- Most instruction occurs either individually, in small (2 to 6 students) or moderately sized (7 to 12) groups rather than the whole class.

- Students help choose and organize the content to be learned.

- Teacher permits students to determine, partially or wholly, rules of behavior and penalties in classroom and how they are enforced.

- Varied instructional materials are available in the classroom so that students can use them independently or in small groups, e.g., interest centers, teaching stations, and activity centers.

- Use of these materials is either scheduled by the teacher or determined by students for at least half of the academic time available.

- Classroom is usually arranged in a manner that permits students to work together or separately in small groups or in individual work space; no dominant pattern exists and much movement of desks, tables, and chairs occurs in realigning furniture and space. (pp. 3–4)

Cuban collected descriptions of over 1,200 classrooms and used other data on an additional 6,000 classrooms as well as data from national studies such as Goodlad's early reports.

Not surprisingly, Cuban found that each time a major reform effort pushed for more child-centered teaching, it had some effect. Some teachers, usually in elementary schools, did give students more responsibility for and control over their own learning.

Cuban is careful to point to the limitations of his study, having focused on observable measures of teacher or student centered teaching to the exclusion of the many other factors contributing to the complex, rich texture of classroom life. He nonetheless feels that his data were so extensive and the patterns of teaching so clear that he can be confident in concluding that we must acknowledge "the persistent occurrence of teacher-centered practices since the turn of the century" (p. 238).

There certainly were exceptions.

> Some teachers, mostly elementary, created their versions of child-centered classrooms where students could move about freely to work in activity centers, where clustered desks made it easy for students to work together, and where teacher-student planning occurred daily. Subjects were correlated and ample time was spent by students working in small groups and independently on projects. (p. 238)

More commonly, teachers knit some of these methods into their dominant teacher-centered mode, mostly at the elementary school level.

> By the 1980s, classrooms were far less formal places for children than a century earlier. Varied grouping procedures, learning centers, student mobility, and certain kinds of noise were acceptable. But far fewer teachers had incorporated teacher-student planning of activities, determination of content, and allocation of class time into their lesson plan. Even less variation was apparent among high school teachers. (pp. 238–9)

Cuban analyzes reasons for the stability of teacher-centered instruction and the less common changes toward elements of child-centered methods and concludes that the best explanation for stability and change in teaching is the power of individual teacher beliefs. Because beliefs are slow to change, teacher-centered methods tend to remain dominant long after waves of reform efforts have washed across the rock of traditional teaching. Because some teachers do change their beliefs about why and how to teach, some change does occur, slowly. (pp. 246–249)

Second, change has been easier at the elementary school level than at the secondary level because of the differences in institutional structures. High schools focus more on subject matter taught to five sections of 30 students segmented into 45-minute periods, so a focus on the child is more difficult and unlikely (pp. 250–251). Cuban combines these two factors of teacher beliefs and institutional structure to construct an explanation for stability and change he refers to as situationally constrained choice (p. 251). He believes this "offers an explanation that accounts for both constancy and change in teaching practice, although the tilt is decidedly toward continuity" (p. 251), as are his data. While institutional constraints were greater in high schools, in elementary schools as well, "Far more stability than change characterized classroom instruction" (p. 253). In spite of institutional constraints on their autonomy, Cuban observed that teachers have freedom to decide many aspects of classroom life central to the teacher/ student-centered instruction continuum, including:

- How the classroom space and furniture is arranged (once portable furniture was installed in rooms)
- How students should be grouped for instruction
- Who should talk and under what circumstances
- To what degree and under what circumstances should students participate in classroom activities
- What tasks are most appropriate to get students to learn what is expected
- What instructional tools (texts, television, film, photographs, radio, etc.) are most productive in reaching classroom goals? (p. 252)

Cuban asserts that the difference between teachers who chose to reject traditional teacher-centered methods and teachers who chose to retain those methods lay in their beliefs:

> The freedom to alter the classroom and exploit that margin increased in those teachers who, for any number of reasons, embraced different beliefs about children, learning, and what schools should do. They believed that those ideas could be introduced to their classrooms and forged ahead in a trial-and-error fashion. (p. 253)

Cuban estimates that 90% of high school teachers retained traditional teacher-centered methods over the years. Others, somewhat more in elementary schools, tried out a few progressive ideas while keeping most aspects of teacher-centered teaching. There was a small third group, "probably in the 5–10% range and concentrated in elementary schools, who believed in progressivism and informal education" (p. 254).

Cuban is optimistic that change is possible in classrooms, within the constraints which exist. In order for change to occur, teachers need to change their personal belief system, he concludes: "Where modest changes have occurred, they have occurred because teachers have absorbed rival beliefs that compete with existing ones. They embraced different ways of viewing the classroom" (p. 262). Only when a change takes place in teacher beliefs about what is desirable for children's growth, can changes in classroom practice follow. Desired goals must precede finding feasible means of achieving them. Otherwise little change will happen, nor will it endure for long.

Implications Of Goodlad's And Cuban's Research

This book aims to promote critical reflection about both the goals of teaching and the methods teachers use to achieve their goals. In order to promote that kind of thinking, the traditional teacher-centered teaching found to be so pervasive by Goodlad and so enduring by Cuban is contrasted to goals and methods of alternative classrooms. The portraits of these alternatives are intended to offer teachers contrasting beliefs and practices, to hold out competing philosophies and pedagogies for their critical reflection. To the extent that these alternative classrooms prompt teachers to re-examine unquestioned assumptions about their own beliefs, to broaden their convictions about the kinds of growth which should constitute their goals, and to recognize the essentially moral basis for their teaching, this book will be justified.

The assumption here is that of Alan Tom's book, *Teaching as a Moral Craft* (1984). Because teachers are given so much power over children who are required by law to attend school, how they use that power to define teacher-student roles and relationships is a moral act, not just a technical decision aimed at efficiency. The hidden curriculum embedded in those roles and relationships powerfully shapes children's self-concepts; enhances or constrains their creativity; promotes either cooperation and solidarity within the classroom community or individualistic competition; nourishes self-direction or dependence; contributes to an internal locus of control or to the expectation that powerful others will shape most personal and social decisions; offers growth of the whole child socially, emotionally and spiritually or focuses more narrowly on knowledge and rationality; and a host of other consequences. The choice of these consequences is a moral choice which demands that teachers go beyond rational reflection to the moral bases of critical reflection; not just comparing alternative educational philosophies and pedagogies, but also personally evaluating them against their deepest convictions and belief systems. It is argued that Cuban is right, that 'teacher change' begins with new beliefs which set new goals leading to methods different from those Goodlad found so widespread and dominant. Morally based critical reflection can be the foundation of those new beliefs.

To help promote such critical reflection, each chapter describes an alternative classroom which offers a critique of Goodlad's traditional schooling. These critiques are intended to help teachers examine the personal consequences to children as well as the societal consequences of teachers' choice of beliefs and practices. They are intended to probe both the curricular implications and the hidden curriculum of both traditional and alternative pedagogies. They should lead teachers to clarify their own convictions about what constitutes the good person and the good society, and what goals for schooling are implicit in those ideals. It is argued that this level of thinking is at the heart of critically reflective teaching, and the chapters which follow are offered to that end.

References

Goodlad, John (1984). *A place called school.* New York: McGraw-Hill.

Cuban, Larry (1984). *How teachers taught: Constancy and change in American classrooms, 1890–1980.* New York: Longman.

Tom, Alan (1984). *Teaching as a moral craft.* New York: Longman.

Chapter One

The Tvind Schools In Denmark[†]

Chuck and Linnie Chamberlin

Introduction

In this chapter, first, the Tvind Schools of Denmark are described, focusing on the aspects most sharply contrasting to traditional schools. Second, these contrasts are used to offer critiques of some common assumptions about teaching and schooling. The chapters which follow will describe a Piagetian school in the Basque country of Spain, a Waldorf school in Sweden, some democratic schools in Sweden observed in 1991–92, and other classrooms in France, the U.S., and Canada.

Development Of The Tvind Schools

The location of the Tvind Program in Denmark is significant because of the tradition of Danish Efterskoles begun in 1851. These were schools for young farmlads, free from any kind of examination, without fixed syllabi, aimed at bringing youth "into a concrete relationship with the practical" (Neilsen,

---

[†] This chapter previously appeared in *Canadian Social Studies*, 27(3), 1993, pp. 115–121.

1991, p. 4). Today 10–15% of Danish students receive their education at private elementary schools (Friskoles) or secondary schools for 14 to 18-year-olds, Efterskoles. Any group of parents and teachers has the right to establish a private school for any religious, political, educational or other reason, with the state providing 50–75% of all educational operational expenses, and granting loans at 4% interest to establish school buildings with no time limit on repayment of loans. The state pays for one teacher per seven students at residential schools. These schools enjoy complete freedom of curriculum, and one teacher joked that the state would even fund a school set up to advocate the overthrow of the state! The average size of the Efterskoles is 80 students, usually living in the school.

In 1968–69 five teachers from Danish schools travelled around the world by bus. They felt they had learned so much from the experience that they decided to start a travelling folk high school for a nine-month course — the Tvind School. They pooled money from their savings, from loans by family and friends, and from state payments. They bought land in Jutland near the North Sea, recruited a group of over-18s, and travelled. From that beginning has grown a group of 36 schools for students from primary to adult levels, plus their own teacher training college. Of these 36 schools, nine are efterskoles, four are international efterskoles with students from various countries who emphasize international travel and service to developing countries, six are travelling high schools, six are household skills schools, and one is a sailing school.

Friskole And Efterskole Academic Program

Danish children begin Grade 1 in the year they turn seven, and the friskole offers the first seven grades of schooling. Since there are no mandated curricula nor state exams, teachers have great latitude in program. However, teachers at the three Tvind friskoles and efterskoles which were observed used the state curricular guidelines in Danish language, math, and English in the morning, using textbooks to structure lessons. Pedagogy was quite traditional with teacher-led discussion and explanation of texts, and several teachers felt this part of their program was quite similar to that of state schools. The main difference was that the small class size enabled teachers to work with individuals and small groups with materials selected as appropriate to their levels. Since friskole classes ranged from 5 to 12 students and efterskole classes only slightly larger, it was common to see a great deal of individual help using texts at different levels.

Teachers in the efterskole often cover a year course in some subjects in half a year, have students take the optional state essay exam, and then focus on other topics. Efterskole students have mandatory homework study from 6:30–7:30 p.m. followed by evening classes from 8:00–9:45 in biology, social sciences and summer theatre. Normally, each teacher teaches a class all subjects, though one efterskole teacher switched physics with another teacher. Afternoon classes are from 1:15–3:15, and are one week blocks on one topic in either history, geography, biology or physics. Hence, topics such as Vikings in the Middle Ages, or Explorers of the Americas, or Magnets or Human Physiology might be the focus of that 10 hours of instruction. However, more integrative topics are common in the afternoons, especially plays, music concerts, and preparation for travel or other big projects. Tvind teachers also emphasize direct experience in these afternoon blocks, going to creeks to sample water, studying their windmill to learn physics, travelling to learn history, geography and culture of Denmark and other countries.

The academic program at the Tvind schools is quite structured — by the teachers, their textbooks, and the projects and travel teachers plan for students. Quizzes and exams give students feedback on their progress. Many of the students have had trouble in state schools, and their parents often feel a more teacher-directed, small-class program will suit these children's needs better.

Big Projects And Travel

A major feature of the Tvind schools programs is involving their students in big projects and travel. The best known of the big projects was the 1975–78 windmill construction project. In protest against government proposals to build nuclear power plants when oil prices soared, the 20 Tvind teachers of Ulfborg decided to build the world's largest windmill to demonstrate how Denmark could develop alternative energy sources rather than nuclear plants. With a half dozen engineers and technicians and many students and adult volunteers they spent three years building a windmill 53 metres tall with blades 27 metres long weighing five tons each. Because they used slipform concrete construction, they had to pour concrete 24 hours a day for 22 days, having set in place 160 tons of steel reinforcing. The machinery pod atop this column weighs 115 tons and is capable of generating 2,000 kw/h. The huge scale of this undertaking, its price of 6.5 million kroner, and the pioneering technology all make this a daunting undertaking, but it powerfully illustrates a central goal of the Tvind school program: children must learn that collectively they have the ability to accomplish ambitious projects if they work hard and plan carefully.

Since the windmill project, Tvind teachers and students have built an indoor swimming pool, planted and maintain northern Europe's largest rose garden with 30,000 bushes; annually rent an auditorium, hire a symphony, and 400 students present massed choirs by Mozart, Schumann, and other classical composers; present summer musicals such as Fiddler on the Roof, Man of La Mancha, My Fair Lady; learn to sail the school's 16-metre sailboat; and collect clothing and other items for the world's biggest flea market in Stockholm to raise money for Third-World projects.

All of these big projects are designed to provide children with experiences of success in reaching high for ambitious projects, developing a confidence in their collective ability to dream big dreams and then working hard to achieve them. This is also modelled for the students by the post-efterskole students who learn Portuguese, then go to Angola, Zimbabwe or Mozambique to help build schools for orphan children, or organize agricultural projects. The teachers also model this "dream big and work hard together" philosophy by mobilizing the resources and expertise needed to buy and maintain a large riding academy, a zoo, a sailing academy, a resort hotel and other facilities now used as residential schools.

The travel projects have been the hallmark of the Tvind

schools from their inception, and every school has a fleet of vans and buses they use to travel to other countries in Africa and Europe. Efterskole students at Ulfborg were in England for two weeks; others were in Rome and Venice; Grade 5-6-7 students at Asserbo Friskole had just returned from Minsk, Belarus; Grade 1-2-3-4 students were writing about their trip to Norway; 7, 8 and 9-year-olds from Veddinge Bakker Friskole travelled around Denmark for two weeks, stopping for a day at the Tvind riding academy at Vilborg. In earlier years students had gone to India, Pakistan, Morocco, Algeria, Spain, Poland, Germany, Lebanon, Iran and Iraq.

Students have numerous responsibilities in the planning and preparation for their travel, and in the tasks during travel, including planning and budgeting for food, for refreshments, for fuel and for pocket money; buying souvenirs; organizing and packing luggage in the vans; cleaning the vans; looking after passports; taking photos; navigation; and exchanging currency. This requires learning many practical skills of group living and cooperation, which is another of the major goals of the Tvind schools that goes beyond the normal academic program. Since students in most host countries don't speak Danish, English is normally the common language, and students in Tvind schools were quite fluent and confident in English by Grade 7. During foreign travel, students stay in the homes of their host school and learn from direct experience the food, manners, customs, clothing, housing, and roles in their families.

Photo, slide and video records of the trip are made, and the Minsk group each had a notebook with a list of 67 questions prepared. When they return, they prepare reports which they present to other school and adult audiences in other towns. Normally each class takes two trips per year for a total of three weeks.

The importance of the travel component is revealed in the commitment not only of large time blocks for the preparation, travel, and reporting, but also in the financial cost. As noted, the schools own and operate their own fleet of vans and buses, and budget 1,200 kroner per student for travel. Rather than spending that money on library or other resources, Tvind teachers always protect this large slice of their budget for travel. If students choose an unusually expensive trip, they will need to raise the additional money to pay for it, as some classes did by selling birdfeed or plants door-to-door. Students also learn to budget carefully so they can have enough fuel and food to get back home.

Learning Through Daily Life
At A Residential School

Because most Tvind students and teachers live at the school, much of the learning takes place as they live and work together outside of classroom time. This means that for 11 months of the year, students and teachers spend from 7:15 a.m. wakeup until 10:30 p.m. bedtime learning how to live, study, work, and play in their school community.

Work

Since Tvind schools hire no janitors, drivers, secretaries, or staff other than cooks and teachers, all of the work has to be organized and done by the cooks, students and teachers. By 7:45 a.m. students are dressed, their rooms are neat and they have set the tables and put out bowls of food cafeteria-style. At some schools, students do the cooking, but at others cooks prepare the food with help from students, who also clear and wash dishes. After morning classes, students spend 45 minutes cleaning before lunch. Some vacuum and clean the rooms, others wash windows, empty wastebaskets, wash vans, weed gardens, clean toilets, clean classrooms, etc. This is intended not only to save money to enable travel, but also to teach children to accept responsibility, work cooperatively, and develop practical skills for daily life.

In addition to the daily cleaning periods, on alternate weekends when students don't go home, they have a variety of maintenance projects at the school, or construction of new facilities. When they bought all the old furniture and carpeting from the Sheraton Hotel in Copenhagen, the building weekend was used to empty their rooms, repaint them, go to Copenhagen and remove the furniture from the hotel, and install it in

their rooms. Roof repair, groundskeeping and other maintenance projects also are designed to help students develop practical skills and responsibility.

Self-Governance

The efterskole has a daily 45-minute meeting to discuss problems and projects, and on Friday have two hours for reports
from committees and grade level problems. Committees have
scheduled time to meet to plan proposals and solutions to
problems before the meeting, and then present reports and recommendations. For example, the landscaping group proposed
a garden, but questions from students and teachers revealed
they had no budget, no study on what would grow well, nor
knowledge of how much space was needed. The principal,
who conducted the first part of the meeting, told them to come
better prepared next week. The welfare committee needed
money for medicine for students, 5,000 kroner for washing
machine repairs, and money to buy a sewing machine. The
cleaning committee objected that the smokers were making too
big a mess and the football players tracked in mud and should
clean their shoes outdoors. The video committee wanted
money for videos now that they'd installed cable to each room
and were hoping to get TVs, and on and on. Two girls, who'd
been laughing at some of the committees, were called up in
front, and the principal asked the 73 students what should be
done. Suggestions varied from having them clean the toilets to
cleaning the pond to singing a song to fixing cocoa for all. The
principal will decide. Other issues had included dealing with
students who'd smoked hash or who had slept together or had
thrown a jam jar out a window on the sidewalk.

The second part of the meeting dealt with problems raised
by grade level groups, and was chaired by one of the students.
During this portion, even the principal had to raise her hand
and take her turn speaking.

Teachers played an active role in the meeting, asking questions which helped reveal how thoroughly proposals had been
prepared, offering comment on proposed punishment (the principal felt some student suggestions were too harsh) and maintaining the rules for running the meeting so the chair could

control sequence of speakers. However, students played prominent roles in discussion of committee proposals.

The efterskole set aside one and one half hours on Monday for the committees to meet and prepare their reports to the Friday meeting. During that time teachers were available for consultation, but did not participate in the committee work. When the welfare committee wanted 5,000 kroner for the washing machine repairs, they could consult the principal and examine the school budget, or when the maintenance committee wanted new locks they could ask a teacher who to phone but were told they must do the phoning and get prices themselves. By setting aside a specific time for the committees to work rather than asking students to use their free time, the school recognized this activity as an important learning opportunity contributing to the educational goals of the school.

By giving students responsibility for planning and presenting proposals, the right to examine the budget and to shift funds, and the right to propose rule enforcement, the school hoped to help students develop skills in cooperation, budgeting, self-governance, conflict resolution, planning and carrying out projects together, and accepting the responsibility that goes with those rights.

Teacher Models

Tvind teachers can choose to become members of the Tvind Corporation which owns the schools, riding academy, sailing academy, vans, windmill, buses, zoo, swimming pools, residences, furnishings and equipment. These teachers are expected to contribute part of their salary to the corporation, to work 51 weeks per year, to live in the residential schools, to teach a small class all their subjects, to organize the cleaning, maintenance and improvement of the school, to do evening counselling and tutoring, to organize concerts, plays, sports Olympics, travel, construction and other big projects, and to spend most of each day living with children at the schools except on alternate weekends when most students go home.

It is also expected that Tvind teachers will be especially good models to the children in their schools. By not drinking, smoking, or using drugs, by living a collective, rather than family life, by working hard, Tvind teachers intend to illustrate to their students that it is possible to choose to live in a way different from others, and that ordinary people have the ability and courage needed to do so.

Community

School grounds have residences where children, teachers and volunteers live. Children's rooms have one, two, or three beds, and teachers have rooms in the children's residences. The communal nature of life for the teachers and students was intensified by the often isolated location of the schools: one on a farm several kilometres from town, one on the edge of a forest, and one at a riding academy on the edge of town. An additional factor contributing to the close contact was the highly organized schedule, assigning tasks within the school for all but a couple of free hours every day. Finally, the close interaction between teachers and children extended from August 1 to June 30, with an optional two-week international summer class in late July, giving 11 months or more of intimate communal life for these small groups of teachers and students. This is seen by Tvind teachers as a key factor in achieving growth in cooperation, conflict resolution, self-confidence and self-governance.

Rules

Tvind publications for prospective students and parents list six rules:

1. You must participate actively in the programme.
2. You must be in the school grounds by 10 p.m.
3. Girls and boys are not allowed to live or sleep together.
4. You may not drink alcoholic beverages at the school, or when travelling to or from the school.
5. You are not allowed to take cannabis or any other kind of drug.
6. You cannot be expelled from school. (Tvind n.d., p. 3)

The first rule may look innocuous, but is the most powerful

of the six. Because the program is so tightly structured for such a large part of the day, and because it is mandatory in its entirety, students' lives are closely regulated and scheduled. One teacher explained that the intensive nature of the school and its success both academically and socially was due to the fact that, "We run them from morning to night." "Run" seemed to have two meanings here, denoting both the rapid pace and the school's control.

Culture

There were other rules as well, such as the prohibition of posters in student rooms. Teachers selected prints of classical art for student rooms, and also selected and put up prints and original paintings in the common rooms. Repeatedly, Tvind teachers said they wanted students to be exposed to the best art, the best music, the best drama as part of the life they experienced, and rejected poster art, pop music, and cult clothing as acceptable parts of Tvind culture. Tvind songbooks offered not only Danish folk music, but an extensive component of songs in English from the union tradition (such as Casey Jones the scab), from the racial equality movement such as, "If you don't find me in the cotton field, look for me in the court house, I'll be voting there," and from African folk songs.

This cultural environment is an explicit critique of pop culture, and sets the Tvind schools in conflict with the international youth culture with its rock music, poster art featuring rock music stars, and "in" clothing and hair styles. Tvind teachers told of students gaining a new appreciation of classical music from their Christmas concert presentation of Mozart and Schumann chorales and masses. But as Giroux (1983) and Willis (1977) demonstrate, such teacher-imposed norms are often met with student resistance, and at Tvind schools students were requesting options between singing and sports and watching TV in their rooms which they could control. Some had small postcard pop posters in their rooms, and used Walkmans to listen to their preferred music. Perhaps the cultural environment at Tvind schools can only offer students an exposure to teacher-preferred culture, an opportunity to compare this culture to commercial youth culture, and the hope that a critique of commercial music, art and drama may at least broaden students' cultural tastes.

Third-World Themes

The principal of the Friskole led discussion of the song, "I'll be voting there," pointing out the tie to the referendum De Klerk had called in South Africa and noting blacks couldn't vote there. Because Tvind operates schools for development workers who spend six months in Africa working on aid projects, and because of the Tvind participation in collecting clothes for the flea market fundraising project, all teachers and students were sensitive to poverty and racism and regularly knit these themes into their projects, discussions and lives. The Tvind schools maintain contact with schools in Algeria, and the Grade 10 class regularly spends three weeks there, experiencing the nature of poverty and Moslem life first hand.

Part of the strong sense of commitment among Tvind teachers is to operate what one teacher called a "people's foreign policy" by avoiding political participation but rather channelling their time and effort into direct people-to-people aid projects such as Development Aid from People to People (DAPP) which operates "child towns" for orphans in Mozambique, Zambia, Namibia, Angola, Zimbabwe and Guinea Bissau. The Tvind Travelling Folk High School on the Road to Victory and their Front Line Institute prepare development workers who work on DAPP projects, building kitchens, showers, toilets, sleeping rooms, classrooms, and offices for their child towns in Africa, or planting fruit trees and vegetables so the towns can be self-sufficient.

Because the Tvind Corporation operates these development worker schools and is strongly committed to helping Africans end apartheid and racism, the Third-World theme crops up in their projects and work with children. The songs they sing, the discussions teachers and principals lead, the fund raising projects they help operate all involve Tvind teachers and children in the struggle to operate their "people's foreign policy" and make Africans more self-sufficient and independent.

The Tvind Schools In Critique Of Traditional Schooling

The program of the Tvind schools offers explicit and implicit critiques of traditional schooling, and may serve as a lens through which to critically reflect on the strengths and weaknesses of traditional schooling. By traditional schooling, the portrait of American schools offered by John Goodlad in *A Place Called School* (1984), will be used. A similar portrait of Canadian schools was presented much earlier by Hodgetts in his study, *What Culture, What Heritage?* (1968).

Critiques

1. Growth of the Whole Person

Traditional schooling places nearly exclusive priority on cognitive development, setting out goals under subject disciplines such as mathematics, science, language and social studies. Because governments set out curricular goals under these subject headings, approve textbooks for teachers to use, and set examinations over the content of these subjects, teachers are pressured to ignore goals of social, emotional and moral development. Consequently, many children who come to school with problems in these areas also experience considerable failure in cognitive development. Since traditional schools tend to ignore the effects on academic progress caused by social, emotional and moral problems, they blame the child for being a poor student. Since they have such extensive curricular content to cover, teachers are likely to feel they don't have time to help their students with these other complications.

Many parents in Denmark give up on traditional schools and send their children to the Tvind schools, knowing that the teachers there must live with the students as well as teach them their subjects. Consequently Tvind teachers must address growth in the areas that most affect social living: social, emotional and moral development. If their students don't learn to be tolerant of those different from themselves, there will be conflict, making teachers' as well as students' lives unpleasant. So teachers plan experiences to build tolerance, solidarity, cooperation, and a sense of right and wrong. The responsibility

23

for cleaning the toilets on rotation is planned to promote cooperation; the lengthy trips and big projects aim at fostering solidarity and confidence; the common meetings that thrash out how to deal with the mess made by the footballers' muddy shoes requires moral judgement as well as skill at conflict resolution; the low teacher-student ratio is intended to enable teachers to individually counsel students struggling with emotional stress.

Living in close proximity for long days and 11-month years demands that teachers recognize the inseparable connections among cognitive, social, emotional and moral development.

2. Significant Knowledge

Students often see the knowledge served up in traditional schools as having no real use in their out-of-school lives, and complain that it's bland, boring, and worthless. Because history is often unrelated to the present and future, because math is often presented as skills needed at the next level of schooling rather than in personal projects now, because students are often told to pay attention even if it's boring because it will be on the test, many students in traditional schools do not see much personal significance or importance in what is in the textbook. Consequently, students without strong home support for school achievement may see little reason to exert much effort in learning the knowledge proffered in text and lecture.

A substantial part of knowledge learned at Tvind is needed in preparation for travel, the presentations which follow, the big projects they plan, fund raising for African aid, major plays, choral music or Olympic sports projects, developing proposals to the common meeting, speaking to non-Danes in English, building and van maintenance, budgeting for planned travel, currency conversion in foreign countries, buying food and fuel, and more. There is intended to be a real life application for much of the knowledge needed by Tvind students that contributes to a positive attitude to learning. The most obvious effect for a visitor is in student fluency in English. While Canadian children with similar hours of formal instruction in French cannot converse with native speakers, many Tvind students from Grade 4 up confidently conversed with adult strangers in English. Knowing that they would regularly travel to non-Danish cities, learning English was not just a school imposed requirement, but an ability they knew they'd have to use next month, and years after. Learning how to read Danish was necessary to find out about Minsk before going there, and to find out the price of food and supplies for the trip. Learning map skills was necessary to plan the route, determine stopover points, and calculate the quantity of fuel needed. Writing and speaking skills were needed to prepare the presentations to other schools about their trip afterwards.

In addition to these kinds of applications of curricular knowledge, Tvind schools intend to also help students learn a wealth of practical knowledge for daily living. This includes how to vacuum, clean toilets, paint walls, build windmills, plant roses, build indoor swimming pools, ride horses, sail boats, comparison shop, raise funds for charity, use commercial dishwashing equipment, lay bricks, prepare slide and video presentations, raise rabbits, chinchillas, goats and horses, among others. The Tvind teachers contend that this knowledge often has more significance in our lives than standard curricular fare such as the causes of the French Revolution or the names of Canada's provincial capitals, and is seen by children as functional rather than academic knowledge.

3. Depth of Understanding

The child reads "Thousands of Ukrainian settlers swarmed to the western prairies to homestead the new land." The teacher hears her pronounce each word correctly and concludes she has read it with meaning. However, words not associated with experience or meaningful context remain empty verbalizations. Textbook and lecture based instruction in traditional schools often leaves superficial understanding at best, and the travel and big project components of the Tvind program imply a critique of the heavy dependence of traditional schools on abstract verbal symbol learning that Goodlad's study found (p. 124).

When Tvind students in Grades 5-6-7 read that Russian shops were empty, they could use direct observation to give it meaning. When they read that Minsk was the capitol of

Belarus, they could relate it to the legislative buildings they had seen. When they read that communist cities were badly polluted, they could compare the air in Minsk and Warsaw to that in Copenhagen. Direct sensory experiences, especially with the culture and geography of other countries, is a key to Tvind children having a greater depth of understanding than is common in traditional schools. The decision to budget more time and money for out of school experience and less time and money for textbooks reflects a conviction about how best to promote depth of understanding, especially among younger children.

This principle also offers a critique of knowledge received passively from text or teacher versus personal knowledge. When children list 67 questions to answer during their trip to Minsk in anticipation of preparing a presentation to other schools upon their return, the knowledge they create is their personal knowledge, constructed from their limited experiences and observations. While some of their knowledge may well be flawed, it is almost certainly going to be more meaningful and usable to them than knowledge passively received in abstract form from lecture and text. The process of actively describing and interpreting their world engages mental efforts likely to produce more substantive understanding than was common in the lessons Goodlad's researchers described.

4. Group Size

Goodlad's traditional school primarily depends on whole-class activities with 25 or so students reading the same text, listening to the same lecture, following the same discussion, doing the same workbook, etc. Tvind teachers begin with classes one-third the common size, possible because the Danish government funds residential schools on a one teacher to seven students ratio. Consequently, they seek a much higher level of active participation for each pupil, more time for individual help per child, and more intensive participation in the learning activity. They argue that their students can learn more in a week than traditional schools because students can't disengage from the lesson in such small groups, and teachers can more closely monitor their participation. As with the time on task studies, Tvind teachers advocate such intensive participation in learning activities that little time is wasted in day-dreaming. As long as traditional schooling is mostly large-group-based, it will be difficult to attain the level of participation Tvind teachers achieve with their students. It will also be difficult to achieve the levels of monitoring and individual tutoring in classes three times as large as Tvind teachers offer.

Combined with Tvind schools' emphasis on knowledge seen by students as significant for use in their travel and big projects, there is a severe critique of traditional schooling for its low intensity, waste of student time in daydreaming, resistance to teacher-chosen lessons, and conflict with other students. Since about 40% of Tvind students are problem children referred by social agencies, and many others are students whose parents sought out the Tvind program because their children weren't successful in traditional schools, this critique of the large class size normally found in regular schools is likely to find a sympathetic response from teachers with large numbers of problem children, and from parents of those children.

5. Social Values and Practices

Readers will by now realize that the way Tvind teachers live offers a clear critique of traditional society, both of the commercial youth culture in the CULTURE section above, and of traditional social life rooted in nuclear families where work is often viewed as a source of income rather than as personal fulfillment. Tvind teachers model other social values and practices in sharp contrast to mainstream society.

First, these teachers' primary group membership seems to lie not in the nuclear family, but rather in their Tvind school teacher group. While income in most Western societies is shared within nuclear families, Tvind teachers pool portions of their individual salaries in order to finance large-scale projects such as purchase of school buildings in the form of a riding academy, sailing school, zoo, and resort hotel in which they reside; purchase of vans and buses in which they travel; construction of indoor swimming pools and gymnasia in which they exercise; construction of windmills and rose gardens; and purchase of extensive camera and editing equipment to make photo, slide and video presentations. They also pool their labor to undertake construction and maintenance projects beyond the ability of individuals and families. They model life without dependence on tobacco and alcohol. They model consensual, collective decision making in which agreement about both program and responsibility for modelling alternative social values and practices is thrashed out.

Unlike traditional schools, where teachers teach curricular subjects as value-neutral, and avoid the controversy necessarily associated with proffering a distinctive alternative life style, Tvind teachers set out to model collective living, and intensive commitment to a seamless lifestyle where work and leisure are inseparable. Tvind teachers intend students to see that life can be fulfilling if the preponderance of their time is used in working hard with others toward collective goals. The brochure put out by the Tvind efterskole partly explains this intent:

> Only Adam (at first) was alone in the world, The rest of us are here together. Fellowship, or collectivism, if you wish, isn't a modern, with-it way of life. At the schools we do not make fellowship the pivot of teaching and living because "we might as well". We make it so because we cannot have a school without it. Profound knowledge of fellowship can be learned only in fellowship, solidarity only by standing shoulder to shoulder. Only many people together can solve problems that can only be solved by the joint efforts of many together. Development is brought about only through the influence of great numbers of people. Generations have learned that the world changes only when many people take a hand in changing it. (Tvind n.d., p. 4)

The principal of a Tvind friskole said one of their goals was to develop in students a sense of community, collectivity, solidarity, an understanding of the ability to meet individual needs within community, accepting the responsibility of solving the problems of self and group. Another goal, she said, was to show students that they can choose to live in a different way from others. One of the qualities of a good teacher, she said, was to lead a life that models good ways to live for children, hoping that these children will want to be like you. In addition to the Tvind schools offering an alternative to the individualism and nuclear family base of mainstream society, they also offer an alternative in terms of expecting full-scale commitment to the projects of the group. Their brochure says:

> You should be forewarned: once you get into your stride, you'll want to do more and more.... There is much work in this, but in return you'll avoid being superficial and half-awake. Travelling with others and writing and talking about experiences and thoughts. Exploring one's own society and taking a stand. Participating in decision-making assemblies' discussions on vital questions. Being able to make music and sing and dance and paint. There is no end to these delights. But you'll have to make the effort. (Tvind n.d., p. 4)

The windmill project symbolizes these two alternative social values and practices. Another Tvind brochure (1988) about the windmill says that they learned that, "People can do anything when they unite about their common future" (p. 6). The windmill was possible, this suggests, because the unique values of collective effort and full-scale personal effort were powerful enough to overcome the many tasks requiring vast resources. Tvind teachers continue to plan big projects and travel that will demand solidarity and intensive commitment for success, thereby providing students with both teacher models for these alternative values and practices, as well as personal experience with them. In these ways, their program provides a critique of mainstream life with its view of a 9-to-5 job seen as solely a source of income; individual and nuclear family life, with the limited projects their slender resources allow; and of a life lived at half-speed, "superficial and half-awake." This stands in contrast to traditional schools which are unlikely to model or to provide experience in a set of social values and practices at odds with those of mainstream culture.

Summary And Conclusions

This portrait of the Danish Tvind schools is intended to describe an alternative to traditional schools, and then to use unique elements of the program as a critique of traditional schooling as drawn from Goodlad's study. The description showed how the Tvind program is marked by concentration on such big projects as construction of a windmill, indoor swimming pool, laundry facilities, rose gardens, and roads as well as two trips to foreign countries each year and major presentations of classical music and musical dramas. However, many of their goals depend on the non-academic experiences of teachers and students during daily life. Practical skills and responsibility are to be learned by having students do much of the work of cleaning and maintaining the school. Learning to accept the responsibility for self-governance is the intent of the common meetings. Teacher models of solidarity, commitment to long hours of hard work, abstention from alcohol and tobacco, Third-World development, and self-reliance offer students an alternative lifestyle. The long hours over an 11-month school year in residential, often in somewhat isolated settings contribute to a strengthened sense of community. Basic rules are set out by the teachers, and preferred art, music and musical drama present students with classical and folk culture.

This description of the Tvind schools suggested critiques of traditional schools as failing to address growth of the whole person, failure to present knowledge seen by students as significant, failure to achieve depth of understanding, use of large group activities that often result in inefficient use of student time, and failure to provide opportunity to contrast mainstream social values and practices against an alternative.

This critique is intended to help educators see that there are substantially different ways to provide schooling to children. Perhaps it will encourage us to critically reflect on schooling as traditionally experienced by teachers and students. Some of the questions the Tvind schools pose to us include:

1. How should we define teaching as a career in relation to other parts of our lives?

2. What areas of growth should be primarily the responsibility of the school, and which should be assigned to family or social agencies?

3. How much of a child's life should be spent in a school and how much at home and in other community institutions?

4. How much of learning should be abstract text-based lessons and how much should be direct experience in non-school settings?

5. In a democracy, what should be the balance between teacher-imposed decisions about curriculum and school life, and student self-governance and self-education?

6. How high a priority should schools place on:
   - international and third-world aid education?
   - experience and appreciation of classical music, art, drama?
   - practical skills of daily living?
   - experiencing and seeing teachers model alternative social values and practices?

7. What knowledge should be chosen for student learning, using what criteria for significance?

8. What physical environments are most appropriate for schooling (consider zoos, riding academies, resort hotels, sailing schools)?

9. For what kinds of students and teachers are residential schools most appropriate?

10. What is the boundary between children learning responsibility and practical skills from working at cleaning and maintenance tasks, and exploitation of the young?

For further information on the Tvind Schools, contact: Hanna Poulson , Tvind Schools, 6990 Ulfborg, Denmark.

References

Giroux, Henry A. (1983). *Theory and resistance in education.* Boston: Bergen and Garvey.

Goodlad, John (1984). *A place called school.* New York: McGraw Hill.

Hodgetts, A. B. (1968). *What culture, what heritage.* Toronto: OISE Press.

Neilsen, Sophie B. (1991). *Meet the Danish efterskole.* Copenhagen: Efterskoles Sekretariat.

Tvind (n.d.). *Tvind: An extraordinary experience.* Ulfborg: Tvind Efterskole.

Tvind (1983). *Tvindpower 1978–1988*. Ulfborg: Tvind.

Willis, P. (1977). *Learning to labour: How working class kids get working class jobs*. Fernborough: Saxon House.

Chapter Two

A Piagetian School In Antzuola, Spain

Chuck Chamberlin

Introduction

This chapter will describe Antzuola school in the Basque region of northern Spain, and its Piagetian program which resulted from a thirteen year long professional development project. This description is followed by a critique of Goodlad's traditional schools, using the Antzuola school program as a basis.

School Context In Time and Place

Antzuola is a town of about 2,500 people in the Basque country of northern Spain. Its public school uses the Basque language to provide instruction to 260 children from age 5 to 14 by 19 staff. The curriculum is set out in general terms by Madrid, and has been in a process of reform for several years, influenced by constructivist and Piagetian principles. The autonomous Basque government funds education and administers programs in both Basque and Castillian languages.

In 1978 some of the teachers of Antzuola were worried about the number of children who were failing at their school, and tried to find solutions. When two psychologists, Manolo

Cainzos and Juan José Kintela came to the school, these teachers arranged for weekly seminars with them during 1979–80. The focus of these seminars were articles by Piaget and by Piagetian psychologists from Barcelona (Piaget, 1941, 1956, 1970; Moreno and Sastre, 1978). During 1980–81 the seminars continued, and teachers began experimenting with some applications of "Pedagogia Operatoria." They also began theorizing about and analyzing their teaching. In March, 1981 they brought in staff from the educational psychology group IMIPAE from Barcelona for a seminar, and in July, 1981 they had a course in Pedagogia Operatoria with IMIPAE staff. In October, 1981 and March, 1982 several teachers went to Barcelona to observe in Pau Vila school where teachers trained in Piagetian pedagogy demonstrated the application of the theories studied. By June, 1982 the Antzuola teachers had written an 80-page proposal for a three-year experiment with Pedagogia Operatoria, which was approved by the Basque government, who provided some funds for further study and application of the ideas introduced by Manolo and Juan José. These two psychologists continued regular seminars in the school, and Juan José was later hired full-time as the school psychologist. Two-year extensions of the school experiment were approved and funded in 1985, 1987 and 1989. During 13 years the teachers and psychologists had worked closely together to develop a theoretical base rooted in readings of Piaget, Rogers, Vygotsky and especially Moreno and Sastre. Teachers had slowly reconstructed the physical environment of the school, replaced the textbooks with new equipment, and redefined the roles of teacher and student in promoting learning and cognitive development.

Physical Environment

By December, 1991, the school had been reorganized into specialized rooms where various kinds of materials were available to children. For children from three to five years old, doors were cut to make their rooms interconnecting so children could circulate freely among specially equipped spaces. In the block room were wooden blocks made by the parents where children were laying out a zoo which they equipped with plastic animals. Piles of wooden and plastic blocks, plain and colored, were everywhere. An adjacent room was called "Plasticos", and small tables displayed a wealth of egg, cereal and other cartons, various glues and paints, shipping cartons, tagboard and papers, tape, string, and a variety of decorations. A third room had low benches around the walls and shelves with commercial and teacher-made games, ranging from parchesi to cards to checkers. A language room had small tables with picture and pop-up books, and floor-level chalkboards. The psychomotor room was equipped with mats and half-meter foam cubes parents had made. On the balcony was a large sand box. A math room had containers of various counters, squares, balances, blocks, and chalkboards. Upstairs the six, seven and eight-year-olds had similar kinds of interconnected rooms.

Grades 3, 4 and 5 were in a separate building several blocks away. Each class had a separate room with hexagonal tables for small groups to work together. The Grade 4 room also had a large table on which a papier maché model of San Sebastian, a nearby ocean city, was being constructed from an aerial photo, books on oceans and fish, an aquarium, scales, and pictures of ocean scenes.

Grades 6, 7 and 8 had home rooms with desks arranged in groups of three, four or five, plus rooms specially equipped for science, plasticos, and technology (equipped with power and hand tools for woodworking and electronics), and a sports field.

Teacher and Student Roles

The children from three to eight years old begin the morning with conversation about their lives outside of school. A group of 11 three-year-olds sat on the floor around a teacher and talked about events at home, similar to show and tell time. The teacher nodded to recognize speakers, but said little. After perhaps a half-hour, the teacher asked them to choose rooms to start in, and they dispersed to the rooms described above, mixing with the four and five-year-olds. Teachers were available to help get materials, observe, sometimes take part in games, and admire finished products.

An important teacher role had been to provide materials and

an enriched learning environment appropriate for the level of cognitive development of their students. Children spontaneously formed their own groups or chose individual activities. Children left one group and moved on to another room and activity when they wished, and noisily chatted with each other about their zoos, towers, robots, shopping bags, puppets, free-form egg carton sculpture, houses, buildings, chalkboard drawings, paintings and games. A group of three four-year-olds played a teacher-made simplified Parchesi game, saying "Bat eta bi son hilu", using the Basque words to add one dot and two dots on their dice. Two seven-year-olds playing checkers were encouraged by a teacher to create their own rules, and they decided a pile three-deep could move any distance in any direction. Five boys about six years old were building a block tower nearly two meters tall, standing atop a table to carefully add blocks to their teetering structure and talking animatedly. Several seven-year-olds worked on their 1.5-metre-tall robot made from food cartons, glue and paint, obviously a long-term project they'd worked on for days.

Afternoons were organized around inquiry into a theme. A 1984 video showed a Grade 4 class in the process of choosing and planning a theme. When the teacher asked what they'd like to study next, suggestions were medicine, ceramics, flowers, fish, confectionery, and horses. For four days groups searched for materials, on these six topics, listed interesting questions and prepared to persuade the class to choose their topic. Then they made presentations expounding the interest and potential of their theme and voted. Ceramics received the most votes, and the teacher asked students to write down things they thought they would need to find out and possible sources, then charted their compilation under subheadings which became the focus of several research groups.

By 1991 this process had been judged to be too time consuming, and broad topics were presented by teachers. The Grade 7 class started a two-week block on Demography in Basque Country, and students formed groups of 2–5 to plan what they would do within that topic. Each group had a planning sheet with five columns. Under "Areas" they listed five or six headings such as Mathematics, Language, Library, Plastica, Science, Technology. Beside each of these headings they filled in their proposed topics and activities. Another column provided space for teacher suggestions. Some students had a separate column for Materials they'd use.

Each group was responsible for locating sources of information and materials needed. This normally meant making phone calls and writing letters as well as using the small school library. During the two weeks following, a ten page report was prepared by each group, along with illustrative products made in the plasticos and technology rooms. The teacher might introduce a specific skill, such as making line graphs, to the whole class or to one or two groups. Sometimes a group would divide its research up for individuals to pursue. But these whole class and individual activities seemed to be less frequent than small group work. As with the younger children, part of the activities for the topic took place in the special rooms equipped for plasticos, science, and technology, where the wealth of concrete materials and tools focused choice of activities.

The role of the teacher still included providing an environment rich in concrete materials and student choices, but also included making suggestions during planning, some direct instruction on new skills, advising on research problems, asking questions to help students anticipate problems, and setting the pace of movement from room to room so all classes could have turns using them. During presentations of the group reports, the teacher also asked numerous questions, offered additional information, and led evaluation of the report.

One teacher recalled that, "The most difficult change, and the one that cost every teacher most effort, was a change of attitude toward the child. The transition was AHH! Hard! To pass from what we were, to listening to the child, to observing the child. If you make a framework of liberty possible, that liberty has risks.... I had to learn how to play with the rules, to learn that I can't always give it to them." If children were to construct personal knowledge from manipulation of the concrete and verbal materials selected by themselves and their teachers, and to talk together among themselves in small groups as they planned and executed their projects, the old ways teachers were used to had to change. Students had to be more active in mental operations, materials had to be more concrete, more open to student interpretation, creation of new ideas, insights and mental structures. Students had to take ownership of the themes under investigation.

In their 1982 proposal to the Basque government, the teachers included a section on their methods, emphasizing that students must select the theme in order to feel that school materials are useful and necessary to attain ends students have proposed. Second, students must manipulate real objects, for only by dealing with reality can children transform it. Third, children verbalize their knowledge, with both their successes and errors, so consequently teachers must present them with situations most adequate for their learning. Fourth, children's graphic representations are an imitation of reality put on paper, but at the same time they are interpretations of this same reality as a function of student interest and developmental levels. Fifth, when one generalizes, one applies what is already known to a new situation, either immediate (without need for reconstruction of previous knowledge) or mediated (when one needs to make an important change from the operational context, requiring a reconstruction). These kinds of thinking need to be promoted by the equipment and social environment of the learning spaces teachers prepare (Antzuola, 1982, pp. 1–2).

Critiques Of Traditional Schooling

Antzuola school's thirteen year long effort to draw on Piagetian psychology in reconstructing schooling offers critiques of both traditional conceptions of continuing professional development programs for teachers, and of traditional schooling for children. Some issues of each area of critique need to be examined.

Continuing Education as a School Project

School systems frequently conceive of professional development as an individual matter, and therefore offer a smörgasbord of workshops, seminars, and presentations available to any teacher in the system. In a profession often described as isolated, individualistic work, with each teacher closing the classroom door to all others, there normally is little opportunity for groups of teachers to collectively take control of the school experience students receive during the seven years of primary school. School staff seldom thrash out a set of learning and teaching principles to guide common pedagogy for their school, nor develop new ways to use their school's space, nor new equipment and materials based on those principles, much less support each other as they risk transforming traditional teacher and student roles and relationships.

The Antzuola experience challenges all of these commonplaces by offering a model of collective, school-based continuing education for teachers. The experience of these teachers in transforming first their knowledge, beliefs, attitudes and goals, and then their teaching practice through collective study, analysis, sharing, planning and evaluation, all repeated over and over in weekly seminars for thirteen years, suggests the collective model of professional growth may have powerful advantages over the individual models school systems often provide.

Central to the collective model are a discourse of shared experience and a mutual emotional support when risking changes. First, this group of teachers set aside time for at least one weekly seminar to talk about what they'd been reading and doing. The thoughts of 15–20 teachers were available to all, with their different interpretations of Piaget's ideas, their varied applications of those principles, different explanations for how children responded to those applications, and the many new ideas for things to try in the week ahead. This pooling of so many different teachers' experiences and thinking over such a long time created a rich reservoir of ideas, strengthening each teacher's understanding of both the theoretical basis of their pedagogy, and the multitude of ways that theory could be translated into materials, activities, questions, roles, relationships and use of space.

Second, the emotional risks that accompany changing basic elements in traditional pedagogy became shared risks, and when the inevitable failures that accompany trying out such innovations were experienced, there were colleagues there at coffee break or lunch or seminar to provide the emotional support essential to persevering. Unlike the individual model of professional growth where teachers come back to their school from a workshop full of new ideas to try out, encounter problems or failures but have no one at hand to encourage them, provide emotional support, or share the frustration with, the collective model has a built in support group who are also struggling with similar problems. While there are certainly strong individual teachers who will persevere in the face of adversity and failures, the immediate availability of a support group seems likely to encourage teachers to persist.

Long-term Collaboration with Resource Persons

The literature abounds with advice that short-term and one-shot inservice programs pay slim dividends in terms of classroom application. Bruce Joyce (1981), Michael Fullan (1985) and others have long noted the need for sufficient time for teachers to grasp the theoretical base of new pedagogy, see it in practice, try out parts of the innovation, get coaching, and refine their new practices. There seem to be two key elements affecting professional growth here, time and resource people. The Antzuola teachers recognized that change in their teaching would require a long time, and wrote a proposal for funding a three-year project, with three more two-year extensions of their program following. The initial recognition that they would need a long period of time in order to make the extensive changes required by Piaget's ideas shows not only a high level of commitment to the ideals they aimed for, but also realism about rates of change. Their initial proposal in 1982 contained long lists of goals in critical thinking, self-confidence, observation and hypothesizing as well as science, mathematics and language, usually expressed in sequential levels of thinking rather than by grade level.

These goals clearly suggest steady growth in independent thinking by children, where the mental process is more the focus of schooling then the final knowledge product. This would demand wholesale changes in the school equipment and in roles of students and teachers. With such fundamental changes as their goals, these teachers recognized the need for years of continuing efforts of trying out ideas, revising, winnowing, refining. Perhaps it was significant that they wrote their first three year proposal after they had been studying and experimenting with these ideas for three years. They had some understanding of the complexity of the problem and the need for long-term goals, plans and resources.

Second, during those thirteen years the Antzuola teachers continuously worked with two trained psychologists as resource people. These two people were key players in sustaining the long term efforts. First, they responded to the problem worrying the teachers, failures of some of their students. By offering help with teachers' problems they enabled the teachers to retain ownership of the professional development program. They were responding to a pre-existing problem teachers had been trying to solve, rather than trying to implement an externally created program. By offering research on children's mental development rather than on how to teach, the resource people cast teachers in the role of having expertise in and responsibility for teaching. Whatever teaching applications these teachers drew from Piaget's work would therefore be their own hypotheses to test, evaluate, and revise. That process would take time, but the resource people, their Barcelona contacts, and the readings they introduced would be there week in and week out over the thirteen years to support the teachers in this work.

Not only would the psychologists offer new ideas from research, but they would also offer support for teachers' efforts to understand and apply those ideas. They said their main role was to provide more massage than message, implying recognition that change in pedagogy demanded as much sustained emotional support as it did new ideas. This cast them in the relationship Massey and Werner (1977) spoke of as mutualism. This sees the resource person more as an access to ideas, rather than a depositor of teacher-proof programs and materials; more of a catalyst promoting integration among readings, teachers, and action research than an expert with preformulated solutions. Because the focus in mutualistic programs is on a process of praxis in which teacher expertise is recognized, protracted time blocks are required during which trust relationships can be developed.

Similarly, Sirotnik and Goodlad (1988) advocate that school-university partnerships need to be long term, focused on problems teachers define, with the resource person's role being to help collect readings and speakers offering relevant ideas. Again, teachers draw on the resource person for ideas to help them create their own solutions to their unique problems in their specific situation, rather than expecting that some generic package will fit, tailor-made, to their needs. This suggests a process over a long time, moving from problem definition to search for ideas to creation of initial hypotheses for pedagogy, to development of materials and activities, to evaluation of first tries, to refinement. The Antzuola teachers and their resource people early made the commitment to such a long term process, recognized the time needed for such a process to unfold, and persevered.

Informed Critical Reflection the Basis for Change

John Goodlad (1984) described the sameness of teaching methods and children's classroom experience in the hundreds of classrooms his researchers visited. His portrait of schooling is of an unquestioned acceptance of teacher and textbook centered teaching methods. Nor is this a recent phenomenon. Larry Cuban (1984) studied school inspectors' reports and other data from eight large school districts in the 1890s on up to recent school reform periods to describe classroom life for children, and concluded that there has been remarkably little change from early teacher-authority models up to the present in spite of billions of dollars and untold hours spent on Progressive Education and New Curriculum programs over the years. He suggests the minimal impact of these efforts lies in the uninspected assumptions teachers make about their pedagogy, and suggests the need for personal philosophies of education to be articulated, against which practice can be evaluated.

The Antzuola experience offers some support for Cuban's conclusions. The two psychologists introduced these teachers to Piaget's theories and research on how children's experiences influenced their development through successively more abstract and formal levels of thinking, and implied that young children needed more experience in manipulating concrete materials and constructing personal knowledge about those experiences than was common in their classrooms. Embedded in the readings and seminars was a new vocabulary about cognitive and operational psychology which provided conceptual tools these teachers could use to contrast the ideal learning environment and pedagogy to that currently used. Consequently, teachers were able to use their new ideals and concepts to critique the teaching traditions they likely inherited from their teachers. Because the psychologists were able to provide readings which provided new ideas from which teachers could develop their own philosophies of education, their own ideals, the stage was set for teachers to use their weekly seminars to critique those traditions. This can be seen as informed reflection, because there was the infusion of new knowledge, new conceptual tools, new vocabulary to use in thinking about their teaching practice. It can also be seen as critical reflection because it was evaluative.

The ideals about children's cognitive development which they now were incorporating into their personal philosophies set the stage for critical comparison between their traditional teaching practices and their new ideals. Their readings had not only provided a vocabulary of conceptual knowledge about children's growth, but also a vocabulary of values, goals, ambitions, and ideals which impelled evaluative thinking about schooling as it was, measured against their new ideals of what it should become. The Antzuola teachers were no less practical in their concerns than teachers elsewhere, and still had to confront the question, "What works?" The difference was that they had clearly articulated ideals offering criteria for what worked, now measured in growth of children's levels of thinking. Cuban suggests this clearly articulated set of ideals is key to breaking out of the decades long pattern of tacit, unquestioned assumptions about teaching.

Growth in Level of Thinking vs. Received Knowledge as a Goal

The critiques above focus on continuing professional development of teachers, and factors affecting their growth. In these last two sections the focus will shift to the teaching at Antzuola School and the implicit and explicit critiques it suggests of traditional schooling as Goodlad portrayed it. Goodlad described teaching as largely transmission of authoritative knowledge. Teachers used lecture, guided discussion, textbook reading, recitation, and examination as methods to transmit knowledge. The states and school systems often set out general curriculum guidelines and topics, and teachers used textbooks, films, kits and other commercial material to provide to students more detailed knowledge about those curricular topics. Often teachers and students were held accountable for that approved knowledge by state, school district or school examinations. This system pressures teachers and students to view the main goal of schooling as the accumulation of authoritative knowledge, rather than development of more formal and abstract levels of thinking and the resulting personally constructed knowledge.

Antzuola teachers used Piaget's work as a basis for rejecting received knowledge as their main goal and instead placed highest priority on "the development of the capacity of the child to engage in mental operations (to operate, in the expanded sense, means to establish a particular type of logical relations among objects and among persons)" (Antzuola, 1982, p. 1). They add that the young child can obtain knowledge about the physical world "by acting on the existing physical world and seeing how it reacts to his actions. At the same time this should mobilize the logico-mathematical structures of his thinking (And that makes them evolve their physical knowledge.)" (p. 9). If the child evolves more complex structures of thinking as a result of manipulating concrete objects, then that will enable "socio-affective development, for the development of language and the construction of all aspects of knowledge" (p. 10). The task of the teacher then becomes to provide "situations in which the material favors the generalization of the ideas required, to test their strength and to avoid the preservation of the answer" by taking into account "the current level of thinking of the child and the level, according to the normal sequence, which follows" (p. 17–18).[1] Thus, for the Antzuola teachers the main goal was to nurture the cognitive development of students by providing situations appropriate to their developmental levels. This is in sharp contrast to the conventional goal of transmitting knowledge set out in curricula and text. The Antzuola teachers aimed at helping children become more capable of independently thinking about their world, rather than presenting students with predetermined knowledge.

In a video (Antzuola, 1984) made by the psychologists and teachers at the school, they chart the levels of thinking Piaget described and some of the differences in how children at each level would respond to problems. They then show children solving problems with concrete materials and verbalizing their thinking and solutions. This emphasizes the Antzuola goal of promoting maximum development in children's levels of thinking rather than in accumulating knowledge, for the sequences intend to show that only by mastering lower levels of thinking can children evolve to more abstract thought. If textbooks present ideas in abstract verbal form, children lacking experiences which have helped them develop the cognitive levels necessary to understand such abstractions will only learn the words, not the ideas those abstractions represent.

Personally Constructed vs. Authoritative Knowledge

Knowledge in traditional schools is often considered valid because it is presented by an authority, either a textbook or a teacher. Textbooks often list several authors or contributors, taking considerable pains to list their academic credentials. University professors, heads of departments, PhDs, or other recognized authorities in their fields are often listed on the title page. Their expertise implies that the knowledge contained in the textbook can safely be accepted as valid, trustworthy, scholarly, and authoritative. When those texts are further presented by teachers to their students as *the* valid knowledge about science, mathematics, history, geography or other subjects, then the message to students is that there is little dispute among scholars about what knowledge is valid and significant. It suggests that the author *knows* what interpretation of events is correct, and that differing interpretations and conclusions (such as those students might make on their own) are misinformed. The relationship between knowledge source (author or teacher) and student is one of authoritative expert and naive neophyte, suggesting the student should passively receive and accept the author's knowledge claims rather than develop personal interpretations and evaluations of those claims.

The Antzuola teachers see knowledge as something each of us actively constructs, and consequently our knowledge will be personal, varying necessarily from one person to another. They offer a constructivist view of what knowledge is and how it comes to be, more consistent with their Piagetian theories about knowledge resulting from the active mental structuring and restructuring of experiences and then verbalizing that thinking in social situations. For these teachers, passive reception of others' generalizations will not result in real understanding, especially for young children in primary school who are at pre-operational or concrete operational levels of cognitive development. Consequently, meaningful knowledge must also be personally constructed knowledge, and authoritative knowledge is quite likely to be only partially understood or even misunderstood.

Further, since their goal is to promote maximum development of children's mental ability, passive receptive learning is counterproductive. Receiving right answers only adds bits of knowledge, rather than stimulation of the active mental structuring of knowledge. The more you press for right answer learning, the more you inhibit the active restructuring process that Antzuola teachers see as vital to the growth they seek. Received authoritative knowledge means giving students the solutions rather than presenting problems with good potential to stimulate active reorganization of mental structures and the creation of more complex personal ideas about their experiences with the world. Antzuola teachers assume the good person is one who is independently capable of constructing personally meaningful knowledge at the maximum level of complexity possible.

This critique of authoritative knowledge cuts at the very core of traditional schooling's hidden curriculum. Paulo Freire (1972) described such schooling as the "banking" concept of education, "in which the scope of action allowed to the students extends only as far as receiving, storing and filing the deposits" so that "it is men themselves who are filed away through the lack of creativity and knowledge" (p. 58). The consequence is

46

that teachers project "the ideology of oppression" through "attitudes and practices which mirror oppressive society as a whole" (pp. 58–59). This ideology of oppression occurs through the learning of roles of teacher authority and student obedience:

> ... the teacher talks and students listen — meekly; the teacher disciplines and the students are disciplined; the teacher chooses and enforces his choice, and the students comply; ... the teacher chooses the program content, and the students (who were not consulted) adapt to it; the teacher confuses the authority of knowledge with his own professional authority, which he sets in opposition to the freedom of the students. (p. 59)

The hidden curriculum in the authoritative knowledge view of teaching is one of minimizing students' creative power and stimulating their credulity, which "serves the interests of the oppressors, who care neither to have the world revealed nor to see it transformed" (p. 60).

Henry Giroux and Anthony Penna (1979) describe the hidden curriculum in an authoritative knowledge approach as the political dimension of schooling:

> Students internalize values which stress a respect for authority, punctuality, cleanliness, docility and conformity. What the students learn from the formally sanctioned content of the curriculum is much less important then what they learn from the ideological assumptions embedded in the school's ... message systems. (p. 28)

Giroux and Penna argue that, "The underlying message learned in this context points less to schools helping students to think critically about the world in which they live than it does to schools acting as agents of social control" (pp. 31–32).

There is evidence of the effect on children of teachers moving away from the authoritative knowledge model and its roles of teachers controlling all the decisions about what to learn, when, and how while the student role is to passively accept the knowledge. Walberg et al. (1979) summarized research comparing traditional teaching to "open education" in which students "are given a degree of autonomy to plan jointly with the teacher the goals, pace, method and evaluation of learning" (p. 182). Of 102 studies on achievement scores, 90 either favoured open education or found no significant difference. Between 85 and 100% of studies comparing open and traditional education favored open pedagogy on measures of creativity, positive self-concept, positive attitude toward school, curiosity, self-determination, independence, and cooperation. These studies suggest that the Antzuola teachers were not only promoting the cognitive development they sought, but were also providing student and teacher roles in which a positive hidden curriculum could flourish. This may be the most telling of the critiques of traditional schooling.

Summary And Conclusions

The teachers at Antzuola School worked with psychologists for thirteen years to learn about Piagetian theory and to transform the school environment, equipment and pedagogy so as to achieve maximum development of students' cognitive potential. Their work suggests critiques of the traditional schooling described by Goodlad in two categories, continuing professional development of teachers, and schooling of children. The participation of the whole school staff in the Piaget project critiques the more common approach of individual teachers pursuing their own interests in isolation from other school staff. Their long-term collaboration with resource persons contrasts with the more common one-shot or short term format. And the emphasis on developing conceptual tools and personal values and philosophy as a basis for change critiques the common "how to" workshops. The Antzuola pedagogy's goal of growth in level of thinking critiques the goal of received knowledge, and their goal of personally constructed knowledge critiques the hidden curriculum embedded in authoritative knowledge.

These critiques raise a number of questions about both the Antzuola teachers' long-term professional development program, and about Piagetian pedagogy:

1. Should some of the billions of dollars and millions of hours now spent on one-shot workshops, teacher conventions, and short-term inservice offerings be used to fund teacher-planned, long-term action research programs? Would children and teachers benefit more?

2. Can resource persons best be used by teachers as aides to their own study of problems in pedagogy, in a mutualistic relationship, rather than as experts with the right solutions to problems externally imposed?

3. Is development of a personal philosophy of education by teachers central to any substantial and enduring change of schooling, or will still more "how to" workshops serve as well?

4. Should the common emphasis on received curricular knowledge continue to be the top priority of schools, or should greater emphasis by placed on the nurturing of Piagetian stages of cognitive development and ability to organize knowledge structures?

5. Should knowledge goals be set in terms of facts, concepts and generalizations selected by authorities in subject disciplines and presented in textbooks and discussions, or in terms of personally constructed knowledge created by students interacting in social groups with an environment rich in concrete materials and experiences?

6. Should the hidden curriculum resulting from teacher authority over most classroom decisions be replaced with one resulting from changing roles and relationships to shared teacher-student responsibility for what, when and how to learn?

For further information about Antzuola School, contact: Sra. Lourdes Etxezarreta Aquirre, Directora, Collegio Publico "Ntra. Sra. de la Piedad" , 20577 Antzuola (Gipuzkoa), España.

FOOTNOTE

1. The translations from Spanish sources are by the author.

References

Antzuola School (1982). *Projecto experimental.* Antzuola, Spain: Collegio nacional "Ntra. Sra. de la Piedad."

Antzuola School (1986). *El pensamiento formal* (video). Antzuola, Spain: Escuela Publica de Antzuola.

Cuban, Larry (1984). *How teachers taught: constancy and change in American classrooms.* New York: Longman.

Freire, Paulo (1972). *Pedagogy of the oppressed.* New York: Herder & Herder.

Fullan, M (1985). "Integrating theory and practice," in D. Hopkins and K. Reid (Eds.), *Rethinking teacher education.* London: Croom Helm.

Giroux, Henry A. & Penna, Anthony N. (1979). "Social education in the classroom: the dynamics of the hidden curriculum," *Theory and research in social education*, Vll(1), 27–40.

Goodlad, John (1984). *A place called school.* New York: McGraw-Hill.

Joyce, Bruce & Showers, Beverly (1981). *Teacher training research: working hypotheses for program design and directions for future study.* Paper presented at American Educational Research Association, Los Angeles.

Marino, Marimon & Sastre, Vilarrosa (1978). *El aprendizaje operatoria como método de estudio del desarrollo intelectual.* Madrid: Alianza.

Massey, D. & Werner, W. (1977). *Alberta education, mutualism, and the Canadian content project.* Edmonton, AB: Alberta Education.

Piaget, J. (1941). *El mecanismo del desarrollo mental.* Madrid: Ed. Nacional.

Piaget, J. (1956). *Los estudios de la psicologia del niño.* Buenos Aires: Lautaro.

Piaget, J. (1970). "La evolucion intelectual entre la adolescencia y la edad adulta," En Delval, J. *Lecturas de psicologia del niño.* (Toma 2) Madrid: Alianza.

Sirotnik, K. & Goodlad, J. (Eds.) (1988). *School-university partnerships in action.* New York: Teachers College Press.

Wallberg, Herbert, Schiller, Diane & Hacotel, Geneva D. (1979). "The quiet revolution in educational research," *Phi Delta Kappan*, 61(3), 179–183.

Chapter Three

Swedish Schools' Student Governance Programs

Chuck Chamberlin

Introduction

Schools in and around Uppsala, Sweden which seek growth in
responsible participation in democratic citizenship wish to provide students with direct experience in the governance of their
most immediate communities: classroom, "cluster," and school.
This contrasts to the teacher and principal directed decisions
portrayed by Goodlad and by Cuban in the Introduction, and is
used as the basis for a critique of such traditional schooling in
the second part of the chapter.

Context Of Time and Place

Swedish schooling normally begins with preschool, then kindergarten at age six, followed by nine years of compulsory schooling. Nearly all students continue on to gymnasium, either into a
three-year academic program leading on to university or technical schools, or a two-year vocational program, soon to become
three years also.

Englund (1986) shows how changing political views of

schooling have changed the goals and curriculum of Swedish schools. The period 1900–1930 was seen as "patriarchal," when the school had a "marked nationalistic, patriarchal character ... (and intended) to paint a favourable picture of the nation, its (well organized) structure and industry, and the foundation on which all this rested, the common interests of employers and workers" (p. 264). However, when political power shifted, parties struggled to change the curriculum to progressive goals and values. This was reflected in a speech to parliament by Hansson in 1928 advocating that the country become a "national home" in which "the strong member does not oppress and plunder the weak, ... the breaking down of all the social and economic barriers into the privileged and the disadvantaged, into those who rule and those who are dependent on them, into rich and poor, land owners and the destitute, plunderers and the plundered" (p. 265).

A shift followed the 1948 School Commission report which advocated "that democratic instruction should rest on an 'objective scientific foundation' "(p. 266). The new schools were to "lay a positive assessment on the value of contemporary science and technology in the service of a welfare society and a reliance on science as a problem-solver. The scientific community was expected to point the way to rational decision making" (p. 267). Rather than the reconstructionist view of citizens who "sustain and help develop democracy," the new teaching materials suggested "citizens were to be a labour resource for building up the prosperity of society" (p. 267).

Englund described a third wave of educational change as 'democratic,' where guidelines for school and adult education were "designed to prepare pupils and students for active participation in society and working life" (p. 270). Education Minister Olaf Palme's policies were influenced by the Swedish Trade Union Confederation, and "as the labour movement became more radical and the power of the unions increased," interest shifted "to those in society with few resources and ... now focussing on distributional questions" (p. 271).

Currently, Swedish curriculum materials such as the syllabus *Lgr 80, General Subjects* (National Swedish Board of Education, 1980) call for junior level study of problems such as "Hazards and difficulties in the traffic environment, making decisions and acting sensibly in traffic" (p. 6); "children's rights in laws and regulations" (p. 9); "Studies of various issues and values which arouse interest" (p. 12); "The fundamentals of democracy, law and justice in school and the local community, framing and obeying rules at home and at school" (p. 13). The goal is social reconstruction to help children:

> ... acquire confidence in their ability to influence and improve their own living conditions and those of other people. The pupils must be encouraged to make their own contributions to the life of the community, and they must be apprised of the opportunities they have of influencing developments by participating in political life and trade union activities and by joining various idealistic organizations and associations. (p. 7)

The syllabus asks that students learn "to seek the causes of antipathies and to process conflicts" (p. 8), reflecting the belief that citizenship in pluralistic democracies requires that we accept responsibility for giving direction to social change through influencing decisions on social conflicts.

In children's materials such as *I Want More* (Gezelius and Millwood, 1985), issues such as a materialist consumer oriented society's impact on the environment and on third-world countries are introduced. Schools are asked to study and *act* on one international issue each year (Blom, 1987).

Clearly, in Sweden the school is recognized to be a political institution used to help shape the nation's future.

Experiences In Democratic Citizenship

While many classrooms observed in the Uppsala area seemed largely similar to those teacher directed ones described by Goodlad (1984), several teachers and principals were systematically involving students in sharing responsibility for making decisions about budget, rules, activities and problems in their schools at three levels.

Classroom Meetings

In Stenhagen and Stordammen schools in Uppsala each classroom from grade one to nine must set aside one hour each week for a class meeting (Klassråd) in accordance with the national curriculum. Anneli Träff is homeroom teacher for 23 seven-year-olds. During lunch Christoffer has come to her in tears because Simon has teased him about how he makes his 4s. Anneli asks if they should talk about it in a class meeting, and he agrees. When students are seated on the floor in a circle to start the meeting, Anneli asks what topics they need to discuss, and notes that Christoffer wants to raise teasing, which she writes under 'Agenda' with his name after it. Farik wants to discuss the amount of homework, and that is added, and another child raises the mess in the lunchroom, while another wants to discuss their gymnastics program. With these four items as their agenda, Anneli asks for volunteers for leader and for secretary, and then reads the report from last week's Klassråd.

One of the problems was that children couldn't hear the recess bell and were late coming back in. Anneli asks if this problem has been solved, and they agree it has. The student leader, Abraham, then calls on Christoffer, who vehemently tells of Simon's teasing. Others speak out, saying it was a problem affecting them because the arguing interrupted their work. Anneli whispers to the leader to ask Christoffer what should be done, and with her guidance Simon apologizes and promises not to tease again.

The student leader calls on Farik who says that having all the homework due on Friday isn't good, that it should be more spread out. Anneli explains that parents say they want weekends left free, so all homework was due Friday, and asks what other students think. Abraham calls on students, all of whom agree with Farik and suggest either less homework, or more spread out, or the option of doing it on the weekend. Anneli asks them to vote on Farik's idea of spreading it out over the week, Abraham counts the votes and reports that three disagree. Anneli asks Abraham to ask the dissenters what they want, and they say they want all homework on Friday. Anneli asks if it's alright to let these three stick to Friday, and all agree.

Anneli notes their time is up, and suggests they continue the agenda next week, and think about the lunchroom and gymnastics problems in the meantime.

The secretary turns in the record of the meeting, a copy of

which goes to the principal.

Discussions with students at other grade levels indicate that similar formats prevail, some rotate the leader and secretary roles, some receive agenda items from the teacher and then solicit additions, and in some cases teachers chair the meetings. Topics discussed reflect the age levels of the students, with more interpersonal problems common at lower grades and plans for school trips and dances more likely in higher grades. Among the topics raised were fundraising for a class trip to Denmark, vandalism, poor food, not enough food, cold food, snacks, hours for their disco, too-easy math texts, class rules, school rules, and use of 500 kroner budget (about $100) for classroom beautification.

House or "Cluster" Meetings

Both Stordammen and Stenhagen Schools have been built with three or six classrooms clustered around a common living-room, and each cluster has biweekly house meetings where two representatives from each class plus a teacher discuss projects and problems. The students take turns being leader and secretary, and add items to a teacher-prepared agenda. Students serve for two months and then new representatives are elected.

Since both schools were new, principals had budgeted some money for houses to furnish their common rooms, and early meetings had mostly been spent looking at catalogs and meeting with sales people. Later problems raised by representatives had been poor food, not enough food, no milk, who will staff the equipment supply room during recess, complaints from marble players about soccer players usurping their space, planning parties and discos, buying magazines for the common room, bringing lamps, posters and games from home for the common room, setting up a cafe, all Grade 7-8-9 students eating in one room instead of in their various classrooms, the need for more playground equipment, objections to the rule about changing shoes when entering school (unchanged), and the need for more interesting books. Some of these problems students were able to resolve themselves, such as bringing things from home to equip their common room. Other problems they convinced teachers or principal to resolve, such as all Grade 7-8-9s eating together. And some they referred to the school's student council, such as food and books.

Because of the way classrooms were clustered around shared common rooms, these house meetings were among representatives of small groups of students at similar age levels with similar interests, factors which keep government close to the students. Their teacher member could suggest who to approach about their problems, and provide the expertise civil servants give to legislators in higher government. The rotation of representatives every two months gave many students an opportunity to experience this responsibility. Grants of some budget amounts gave the committee resources and responsibility for their use, for which they were accountable to not just their own classroom, but to a larger community. Thus, the house committees were designed to provide experiences similar to those of municipal governments who receive some of their resources, and responsibilities, from senior governments, and must sometimes lobby there for help.

School Councils

Each school elected two delegates from each house to the school council, which elected a chair, vice-chair, secretary and treasurer. Problems and projects which can't be satisfactorily resolved by class or house meetings make up the agenda at their monthly meetings. A teacher advisor attends and can suggest agenda items, as well as where to go for help.

Food was a major issue, and the Stenhagen council was particularly concerned about lack of milk in lunches. Their meetings with the school cooks had been fruitless, as they said there was no money for milk in their budget. To protest, three girls would not eat. The principal suggested the student council meet with the federal government member to press for more funds, and they were trying to arrange the meeting. However, some students said nothing would be done, the adults don't listen to kids, "They look down on us."

Stordammen school council also had received many complaints about food. Moslems were served pork, and some dishes were sent back to the kitchen untouched because no one liked them. Student council gave each student a list of dishes to mark ones preferred and disliked. A food committee collated the replies, took the recommendations to the cooks, and were able to get them to ask central dietitians to change what could be served, thereby ending meatball fights. Now the food committee meets with the cooks each month to plan the monthly menu. The student council chair is worried cutbacks will mean loss of milk here also, but felt they could phone and write the government to keep milk funds, or demonstrate if necessary.

Part of the chairperson's confidence was based on council's struggle to get books for their empty library. Their new school opened with no library books, and they met with school officials to no avail, then invited parents, teachers, and students to a demonstration at the school, to which the Uppsala government member was also invited. Eventually some of the promised books were forthcoming. The students had learned that if they were willing to get organized, put in the time and effort needed, and persist that they could make their school a better place for all.

Other issues school committees had discussed included funding discos, which company to choose for class photos, selling school tee shirts to raise funds, the school's May carnival, increasing the number of basketball hoops, and the right to buy snacks on breaks.

Classroom Learning Activities

In addition to the formally structured school governance programs noted above, each school also had a variety of classroom provisions for letting students share responsibility for decisions about learning activities. While some teachers used mostly whole-class teacher directed methods, others gave students a great deal of control over their learning. Grades 7-8-9 at Stenhagen school had six hours per week for independent research in Swedish, social science and nature. Their teachers have boxes of materials on a dozen topics for students to choose from, or students can choose their own topic. Sample projects had included a computer painting and report on Egypt; essays on grammar, forests, the federal election, Sumeria; and a chart on a Swedish artist. Students can either work alone or form their own groups. Each day they record in their diary what they did that day on their project, and what progress they made on their final presentation, which may be an essay, chart or other product.

Anneli Träff has her seven-year-olds work individually during their daily 40-minute math block. Each student has a sheet listing a variety of math materials in the room: math book, clock, measuring length, measuring weight, measuring volume, money, games, jigsaw puzzle, cards, geometry, and tangram shapes. When students have written in the number of the math book page they've completed and two other activities on the list they meet with Anneli to get any explanation needed for the next math book page and review the pattern of their week's choices. This gives students some control over their workpace, materials, choice of activity, sequence of activity, and whether to work alone or in a group. It also frees the teacher to provide more help for some children than others, to monitor and give feedback on their work, to provide a variety of materials at different levels, and to help students become more independent, self-directed learners.

Christer Bermheden teaches English to students in Grades 7-8-9 at Stordammen School. He uses a method he calls 'autonomous learning.' He begins in September by explaining to his students what researchers have learned about how to learn a second language, reviewing Krashen's acquisition theory. Then he provides them with a textbook, and workbook, and access to audio tapes. They are given a planning sheet which specifics a section of their textbook and three columns: *Date*, *What I will do*, and *Homework*. Students select study partners and look over the section of text, then fill in the 'What I will do' and 'Homework' columns for each date. The time blocks are three to four weeks long, giving students considerable latitude in their planning before the test on the last day. For the grade nine students, one of the four weeks was to be a textbook-free reading week where students could choose from various English books for free reading. Each class ended with five minutes for a diary entry on what they had done and learned that day. While Christer did use some time at the beginning of some classes to play tapes to the whole class, the bulk of time was student planned by study groups, and the teacher's role was to answer questions, monitor and correct, write responses to diary entries, provide resources, and structure the content. These students, like Anneli's, had the freedom and responsibility for deciding on grouping, workplace, learning activities, homework, some materials, use of teacher, and daily diary self-evaluation.

Other teachers provided gradations of student sharing in decisions. A drawing teacher selected medium (oil, charcoal, clay, etc.) and focus (perspective, shadow, etc.) and then let students decide what to create. A gym teacher had some free days for students to decide what to do, and other times lists two or three activities for students to vote on. A social science teacher introduced the topic Free Churches and let students choose any church outside the official Church of Sweden to research and write a report on. A grade five teacher puts the assignments for the day on the board and lets students organize their time themselves. Some student texts have basic and advanced sections, and students can choose to go on to the advanced sections or not. Students in Grades 7-8-9 also have options, and can select from French or German, computer or handicrafts.

Combined with the formal student government structures, these classroom learning activity decisions give students from grade one to nine in the compulsory schools extensive experience in making group and individual decisions and seem likely to build democratic expectations about their roles and their relationships with those in authority positions.

Critiques Of Traditional Schooling

In 1916 John Dewey argued in *Democracy and Education* that the classroom community was a microcosm of society. Since then, many studies have probed into the question of how schools and society are connected. In 1976 Bowles and Gintis in *Schooling in Capitalist America* presented evidence that a hierarchical economic system shaped hierarchical schooling and offered a theory of correspondence between the two. However, Carnoy and Levin (1985) in *Schooling and Work in the Democratic State* argue that counterpoised against hierarchical capitalism is egalitarian democracy, leaving schools as arenas of struggle between capitalist and democratic forces. The portrait of schooling drawn by Goodlad's (1984) study of 1,350 teachers and their 17,163 students based on detailed classroom observation points to classroom microcosms not of a democratic society, but rather of an autocratic society. The daily classroom experience for children is whole-class teaching where lecture, recitation, text study, independent written assignments and quizzes are all controlled by the teacher, leading Goodlad to conclude, "the domination of the teacher is obvious in the conduct of instruction" (p. 123). Consequently,

> Students in the classes we observed made scarcely any decisions about their learning, even though many perceived themselves as doing so. Nearly 100% of the elementary classes were almost entirely teacher dominated with respect to seating, grouping, content, materials, use of space, time utilization, and learning activities ... in 90% of junior high and 80% of senior high classes. (p. 229)

While one out of seven students reported being involved in school government (p. 224) such heavily directive teachers as described above are unlikely to offer much significant power to students there either.

Against Goodlad's data and portrait of American schooling, the Swedish schooling described above offers several critiques.

I

Authoritarian And Democratic Models Of Good Society

The school is a socially constructed institution serving goals set by the society it serves. Among those goals are preparation for citizenship in that society. Some societies, such as China's, systematically use propaganda, Young Pioneer youth groups, and authoritarian classroom structure to prepare students to fit into their centralist, authoritarian political system (Chamberlin, 1986). There is a congruence between the real political structure of the state and the roles, relationships and norms learned by living in classroom and school communities. In other societies there are degrees of incongruence between democratic conceptions of the state and authoritarian community life in schools. The schooling Goodlad described seems more appropriate as preparation for citizenship in an autocratic state than in a democratic one.

George Wood (1984) describes two conceptions of democracy and their implications for schooling. In representative democracy, citizens elect leaders every four years and then go on about their daily lives, leaving governance to those chosen. In participatory democracy citizens feel responsible for continuing participation in political affairs. Wood argues that a society is democratic only to the extent that all citizens have, and feel that they have, equal opportunity to participate in sociopolitical decisions. This requires not just choosing leaders every four years, but also continuing to exert influence on decisions those leaders make. This in turn requires that schools develop students who are confident in their ability to exert influence on political decisions. Since adults with a low sense of political efficacy also have low levels of participation in the political arena (Massialas, 1978), the school designed to prepare citizens for a participatory democracy must find ways to develop this confident self-concept. Ehman (1980) concludes from an extensive review of research that "the more participant the school, the higher the students' political efficacy" (p. 111) and that an open classroom climate "in which students believe that they can influence the rules and working of the classroom is related to student political attitudes" (p. 113).

With this conception of the differences among education for citizenship, in authoritarian, representative democracy, or participatory democracy in mind, the contrast between Goodlad's portrait of teacher dominated classroom life and shared teacher-student decisions in the Swedish schools described above becomes socially significant as well as personally so. The Swedish state has specified school responsibility for providing students with experiences in participatory citizenship as preparation for adult citizenship in an egalitarian democratic state. The schools observed have provided structures, money, and influence to students, and students have come to expect to share in decisions both about their learning activities and about governance of their classroom, cluster and school. This model of citizenship education seems aimed at a participatory democratic state, and serves to critique autocratic classroom life more suited to citizenship education for an autocratic society.

II

Ethically-based Decisions And Actions

Some teachers believe that young children have not developed the ethical and moral maturity needed to share in making decisions in their classrooms and schools, and therefore the responsible adults (teachers and principal) must retain control over decisions about rules and pedagogy. The classrooms studied by Goodlad, with their heavy dominance of teacher control over all decisions, reflects such skepticism of children's development of responsibility.

However, the Swedish schools' examples offer a critique of this unwillingness to share control over decisions with children, drawing on theory and research on children's moral development. Kohlberg (1969) drew on Piaget's work (1965) to devise a theory of stages of moral development, and used his theory as the basis for designing a "just community" program for schools (1975). Working with parents, high school students and teachers, Kohlberg set up a just community school in which the students:

> ... had democratically decided at its meetings to pass certain rules and work toward certain goals. These included rules about not stealing, not cutting classes, and not using drugs or alcohol during school hours ... (and) to increase integration among black and white students. (Reimer, 1981, p. 487)

Over the four years of the just community school program, students came to take increasing responsibility for setting the collective norms for the school and for maintaining those norms and expectations. Reimer's study showed that there was "a progression in the level of expectation from the early to the later years. This progression indicated an increase in the taking of responsibility by the students" (p. 487). Further, when students' levels of moral judgment were compared, over one year, to students who had discussed hypothetical moral dilemmas instead, the just community school student's levels of moral judgment increased among 60% of students versus 30% in the hypothetical discussion group, leading Reimer to conclude that the program did produce "changes in judgment in addition to positively affecting student moral behavior" (p. 487).

If teachers wish to help students grow in their ability to make morally and ethically sound collective decisions, and to act on those decisions as well, then the "just community school" project and the Swedish schools projects suggest the value of teachers giving students more responsibility for governing themselves and for making classroom decisions about what to learn and how to learn. Traditional schooling, with its teacher control over these decisions, may prevent students from having the kinds of experiences in governing their communities needed for the development of ethical and moral judgment and the collective action based on that judgment.

III

Social Justice Versus Elitist Society

Newmann (1975) argues that the key principle of democratic government is consent of the governed. Central to Newmann's argument is the ethical importance of equality, based on the moral premise that every human being is entitled to respect and dignity. Dignity, Newmann asserts, is possible only if the claims and interests of each person are treated impartially, which in turn requires that society be organized so that power is distributed as equally as possible through rights to participate in periodic selection of leaders and direct participation to affect the outcome of specific issues. This emphasis on equal access to power minimizes the chance that equal rights can be violated. Newmann concludes, however, that the consent ideal is not being realized, and that "education is, in part, responsible for its failure" (p. 46). He cites Verba and Nie's study, indicating that 11% of citizens are extremely politically active and 47% are relatively inactive, and that "high participators are overwhelmingly upper-status, wealthy, white, middle-aged citizens taking a 'conservative' stand on such issues as welfare" (p. 50). Further, Newmann reports, government leaders in the Verba and Nie study:

> were more responsive to active than inactive citizens. That is, they were more aware of the activists views, tended to share those views, and spent more of their efforts trying to implement them. Views of the inactive citizens were not as consistently known, shared, or pursued by government leaders. (pp. 53–54)

The picture which emerges is one of an elitist society in which "upper-status, wealthy, white, middle-aged, conservative" citizens are politically active, and are listened to by government leaders, while the poor are passive and don't expect to be able to extend any influence.

The children in the elitist families are likely to learn a sense of political efficacy, or confidence in being able to influence community decisions, from seeing their parents confidently pick up the phone and invite the mayor to lunch at their country club to discuss changing the zoning on residential land they own to commercial zoning. Children from poor families are more likely to learn from their parents that "you can't fight City Hall," so why waste your time trying.

The schools Goodlad describes, by providing children with 13 years of experience in autocratic governance, teach passivity rather than active participation, and only students who learn at home to expect to be effective activists are likely to develop confidence in political participation. In this way, the failure of schools to develop a sense of political efficacy in all students, rich or poor, black or white, supports the continuation of an élitist society. The Swedish schools aim to give all students experience in self-governance, and thereby to develop confidence in all students' ability to effectively participate in adult citizenship activities. These schools intend to contribute to social justice rather than to the maintenance of an élite society.

Summary And Conclusions

The Uppsala schools' student government programs offer an alternative to preparing students for citizenship in a democracy. Their trust in students' ability to learn to accept responsibility for collective decisions reflects belief in a version of democracy which assumes active citizen participation in setting policy, not just in electing representatives. It also offers opportunity for moral development so that trust can be increased over the years. This alternative presents several critiques of traditional schooling and raises such questions as:

1. Should the ideal democratic society be one of active citizen participation or of a representative form?

2. Should schools provide experience in self-government on "active citizenship" lines, or on representative form lines or focus on the academic study of democracy?

3. Is development of a more socially just society an appropriate goal for public schools?

4. Should moral development as sought in Kohlberg's "just community" school program be an important form of growth for our schools?

5. At what age can teachers trust children to begin making responsible decisions about classroom goals, rules, and learning?

6. What should be the relationship between the adult professional teacher and the young 5–12 year old child in classrooms and schools concerning the making of decisions?

For further information contact:

Elizabeth Olsen, Chef   *Ann Christian Lindborg, Chef*
Stordammen Skole   *Stenhagen Skole*
S75002 Uppsala   *S75002 Uppsala*
Sweden   *Sweden*

References

Blom, Margot (1987). "Citizenship education in Sweden," a paper presented at the National Council for Social Studies Annual Meeting, Dallas, Texas.

Bowles, Samual & Gintis, Herbert (1976). *Schooling in capitalist America.* New York: Basic Books.

Carnoy, Martin & Levin, Henry (1985). *Schooling and work in the democratic state.* Stanford: Stanford University Press.

Chamberlin, C. (1983). "Knowledge + Action = Citizenship," in Parsons, J., Milburn, G., & Van Manen, M. (Eds.). *A Canadian social studies.* Edmonton: University of Alberta.

Chamberlin, C. (1986). "Political education in Heilongjiang, China," *New Education,* 8(2), 23–35.

Cuban, Larry (1984). *How teachers taught: Constancy and change in American classrooms, 1890–1980.* New York: Longman.

Dewey, John (1916). *Democracy and education.* New York: Free Press.

Ehman, Lee (1980). "The American school in the political socialization process," *Review of Educational Research,* 50(1), 99–119.

England, Tomas (1986). *Curriculum as a political problem.* Uppsala: Studentlitteratum.

Gezelius, H. & Millwood, D. (1985). *I want more.* Stockholm: Swedish International Development Authority.

Goodlad, John (1984). *A place called school.* New York: McGraw Hill.

Kohlberg, Lawrence (1969). "Continuities and discontinuities in childhood and adult moral development," *Human Development,* 12, 93–120.

Kohlberg, Lawrence (1975). "The just community school: The theory and the Cambridge school experiment," in Kohlberg, L. (Ed.) *Collected papers on moral development and moral education,* vol. 2. Cambridge, Mass.: Center for Moral Education, Harvard University.

Massialas, B. (1978). "Political socialization and citizen competencies: A review of research findings," in *Behavior variables related to citizen education: Colloquium papers.* Philadelphia: Research for Better Schools, Inc.

National Swedish Board of Education (NSBE) (1980). *Lgr 80 general subjects.* Stockholm: NSBE.

Piaget, Jean (1965). *The moral judgment of the child.* New York: Free Press.

Reimer, Joseph (1981). "Moral education: The just community approach," *Phi Delta Kappan,* 62(7), 485–7.

Wood, George (1984). "Schooling in a democracy: Transformation or reproduction?" *Educational Theory,* 34(3), 219–239.

Chapter Four

Red Deer Social Action Project

Rick Moore, Don Taylor and Chuck Chamberlin

Introduction

Don Taylor and Rick Moore were teachers in Grade 5 and 6 in Red Deer, Alberta in the summer of 1982 when a mosquito outbreak drove people indoors and a petition was started by a woman to increase the level of chemical spraying in the town. Don and Rick introduced the issue to their classes with a dramatized family argument (around a backyard barbecue) over whether to spray the mosquitoes or not. The sides of the issue became clear, and the teachers' insistence on evidence to support arguments led directly into a session where parent group leaders worked with small groups to list some of the things they'd need to learn about to resolve the issue.

Developing The Social Action Project

Don and Rick described the next step as follows:[1]

> With the issue clearly established and research questions listed, we moved into small-group study of issue components. We feel that the idea of breaking the class into small groups in order to

pursue different aspects of the issue more thoroughly is important and worthwhile: It should be included in projects such as this. However, the Grade 5 students didn't do as well as the Grade 6 students in this aspect of the project. The Grade 6 students put some extra initiative into their research. Telephone calls were made to doctors, to the golf course, and to Dr. Bruce Taylor of Alberta Environment. The students thought pretty carefully about the questions they wanted to have answered.

They needed guidance along the way to find the resource people, to make sure they were asking questions pertinent to the subject, and to get their information down effectively on chart paper. A lot of maturity and independent work was expected in this area.

A second aspect of gathering and organizing data was the use of learning centres. On the whole, we felt our learning centres were beneficial. They gave students the opportunity to gain issue information that assisted them in making a good culminating decision. There was a wide variety of activities. Attempts were made to provide other than solely print information. Sharing materials between the Grade 5 and 6 classes worked well as we used reserve cards. We used a chart to record successful completion of activities by each student.

Guest speakers became very important sources of information for the students. Janet Chiasson had initiated the pro-spray petition, and stated her point of view strongly. Mayor Bob McGee explained how the decision-making process worked in Red Deer, how students could get items on Council's agenda, and encouraged them to feel open and forward in approaching Council. Dr. Bruce Taylor, head of the Biting Fly Control Division of Alberta Environment, gave information about all sides of the issue. Bruce's colleague, Jack Harlos, led the class through a pond study, finding mosquito larvae and a host of predators of these larvae. He opened students' eyes to the "biological control" solution.

This led into lab studies, raising mosquitoes from eggs to adults, and experimenting on their reaction to heat, cold, light, and sound. In turn, a case study of the effects of draining a slough revealed the broader ecological effects. A dress-up role play of aldermen meeting with townspeople holding differing views helped show how the democratic process worked, and helped students appreciate opposing views. It helped bring out all sides of the issue and the full range of consequences to consider. Don and Rick describe some of the activities:

Decision Map and Declaration of Position

After the preceding activities were completed, students were asked to use the "Decision Map" to summarize the issue. The Decision Map was very worthwhile, partly because it caused students to focus on information, weigh the pros and cons, examine their value positions, and then make a decision to be adhered to even when challenged. Also, the Decision Map is something that students can, and hopefully will, use in any other investigations that may be done.

Following the completion of the Decision Map, students wrote a composition explaining their position. They declared their position orally in order that the rest of the students could see with whom to align themselves. One problem that we observed was that some students declared their position but, upon hearing the information of the other students, switched their viewpoint. This is unfortunate, but sometimes adults do the same. We offer two recommendations for decision making. First, before beginning the Decision Map, be very sure that all of the important points have come out for discussion. Then stress the importance of making the best decision possible. Second, post people's position papers publicly in order that people can review them easily.

Actional planning was based on the model presented in Hungerford's *Investigation and Action Skills for Environmental Problem Solving*. The Hungerford model was very useful in this aspect of the project in bringing out and explaining just what action was. When we began talking about persuasion, students realized that both logical and emotional appeals could be effective in helping to change people's opinions. Most students undertook some form of a persuasive project to encourage others to think the way they did on the issue. Some students made up pamphlets, posters, songs, and skits, talked to neighbors, and wrote letters to the editor of the local newspaper. We touched on consumerism and legal action, but because they were not really very applicable to students, we did not dwell on these issues. Political action, however, was our main thrust and the climax of our whole mosquito project.

We intended to involve parents heavily as group leaders and coordinators, with the political action aspect. We held a parents' night with the students to discuss political action. The idea was to begin formulating strategies for each group's presentation to City Council. The no-spray group opted for a poem to express its feelings. The biological control group decided to put on a demonstration of how natural predators could feed on mosquito larvae. The pro-spray group wanted to produce a slide-tape presentation in order to get its message across.

The parent volunteers were not as plentiful as we had hoped. In fact, one group did not have any parents in it, so Rick jumped in and provided the leadership for a good presentation. We think that the lack of parent helpers may possibly reflect the apathetic feeling many adults have toward getting involved politically. Because they think their actions are futile, they have no reason to get involved. The actual presentations to Council on June 13 were all great, and we felt very proud of what the kids had accomplished over the four and a half months of the project. After hearing the presentations, Council immediately moved a resolution to undertake a study to determine the extent of the mosquito population in the Red Deer area and to look at possible ways of dealing with it. So we feel we were very successful with our political action. The kids found out firsthand what it's like to research carefully an idea, gather the facts, make a decision as to one's personal position on the issue, design an appropriate means to communicate desired direction to the affected decision makers, and get some results. We are very pleased with the whole project and feel that all the effort was definitely worth it.

In fact, Council acted on the report, extensively shifting from chemical spray to use of predators, and the students' efforts were rewarded.

Part of the experience was learning to use the media to influence the community. Through letters to the editor, public meetings, and appearances on local TV talk shows, students were able to place the issue in high profile. Don Taylor noted that since students had seen newspaper write-ups, they realized they could create news and contribute to community awareness. "They learned they could use the media to get across their ideas," Don said.

Similarly, the experience of making presentations to city council seemed to change the way students thought about themselves. Parents felt that their children "Had good reasons for taking the positions they chose. It's helped their decision making, to weigh all different sides and make up their own mind." "I was impressed with how well they analyzed the different aspects, the social issues, the environmental issues. I thought that was beyond them, but they seem to have done quite exceptionally well." "It's evident she handles herself quite confidently in talking about this particular issue. It's helped build up her confidence from that type of experience."

The teachers felt the main effects on their students were an appreciation for the complexity of social issues and the need for systematic research to resolve them. Learning to use a decision-making process was important. Rick felt his Grade 6 students had learned to be more assertive and confident, and that the political arena is not to be feared. Don felt his students now realized they were citizens too, with the rights and responsibilities that includes.

On a questionnaire students completed, they were asked if they thought they could do anything about an unfair school rule. One student said, "Now that I've spoken to Council, I think I could try to do something." For some at least, there did seem to be growth in confidence, a sense of citizenship, perhaps more assertiveness.

The Red Deer Project As Critique Of Traditional Schooling

1. Personal and Social Relevance

Goodlad (1984, p. 126) pointed out that students seem to see no relevance to their lives of textbook knowledge learned for tests. Consequently, "Teachers and classes appeared to occupy positions of declining significance in the lives of the young." They feel bored to death by having knowledge presented with only the justification for learning it that it will be on the upcoming test. The Red Deer project contrasted sharply to Goodlad's schools on the relevance criterion. Because the issue was local, they directly experienced it, heard their parents discussing it over supper, felt the bites at soccer matches, and quickly recognized both the personal and the social relevance of the issue. It was apparent to each child that the choice of solution would have direct impact on their lives and their community.

The fact that this was a contentious issue, with environmentalists hotly supporting one solution and some mothers of young, housebound children circulating a petition to support another solution also added to the relevance of the knowledge. Even after students had studied the problem for over four months, and had amassed extensive information on the environmental, health, social, economic and recreational consequences of the alternatives, there were still a number of students torn between the solutions, wanting additional information to help them decide. The knowledge wasn't needed for an exam, it was genuinely needed to help make the best decision possible on an admittedly complex issue.

When the date was fixed for their city council presentation, even more relevance was given to the knowledge sought. Now it wasn't just a matter of helping them individually make a difficult decision, but they needed to look credible, informed, and responsible in the public glare of the city council spotlight. Further, they were to be advocates of a preferred solution, so they needed knowledge to enable them to build a strong case based on evidence. Relevance was gained from the social action component being included. Don Taylor said that his students felt like responsible citizens now, and *needed* knowledge to assume they'd be seen publicly as responsible. The social action component, then, strengthened both the social and the personal relevance of the knowledge sought.

2. Integrated Knowledge

Goodlad pointed out that knowledge in school is normally organized in separate subjects labeled science, math, language arts, or social studies. Curriculum guides, syllabi, textbooks and exams set out the broad outline and some of the details of what is to be "covered" in each subject.

Goodlad concluded that this division into subjects "encourages a segmented rather than an integrated view of knowledge" so that "what students are asked to relate to in schooling becomes increasingly artificial, cut off from the human experiences subject matter is supposed to reflect" (p. 266).

In contrast, the Red Deer project began with a local issue to be resolved. The knowledge needed to make a good decision was not predetermined by curriculum or textbook authors, but rather emerged as students wrote letters to Alberta Environment, interviewed the mayor, invited a petition organizer to talk with them, held public meetings, did pond water studies, read brochures from the Biting Fly Control Division, did simulations, read newspaper and magazine articles, phoned civil servants at city hall, watched films, and steadily added both new knowledge and new questions. The knowledge boundaries emerged during the study as people and resources added new dimensions neither the teachers nor students could have foreseen at the outset.

Nor did this knowledge neatly fit within subject disciplines. To think of this as a Science project wouldn't leave much room for the extensive knowledge gained about economics, government, recreation, aesthetics, and ethics. The artificiality of traditional subject disciplines becomes clear when this type of real world issue becomes the focus. Knowledge becomes legitimate not because experts in the disciplines say so, or because you'll need it to understand the concepts planned for next year, but because it is *useful* in resolving pressing issues of personal and social relevance. The pragmatism of the knowledge is clear to students, unlike predetermined curricular and textbook knowledge.

Similarly, the wide range of skills students needed weren't taught as language skills such as listening, taking notes, interviewing, phoning for information, and writing a formal letter or social studies skills such as using an index and table of contents, interpreting graphs and maps, and identifying bias, or science skills such as observing, recording data accurately, hypothesizing and so on. Rather than being taught in separate subjects in isolation from any genuine need to apply them to a problem of immediate personal concern, these and a much wider range of skills in research, communication and persuasion were learned when needed to further students' inquiry.

Again, as with the knowledge, these skills gained legitimacy in the school program not on the basis of adult experts saying so, but rather because students saw that they needed proficiency in them in order to resolve their issue and take responsible social action on their decisions.

3. The Good Person, The Whole Child

Goodlad noted that school goals are often aimed at developing the whole child, a well rounded good person, with development of idealistic and altruistic ends in social, civic, cultural and personal domains. However, he concluded that schools "were contributing minimally to such goals" (p. 239). Indeed, he concluded schools contributed negatively to some of these goals. Often it seems these non-knowledge goals slip between the cracks of the traditional knowledge and skills defined as curricular subjects.

Yet, when parents were interviewed at city hall after their sons and daughters had made their presentations to mayor and aldermen, they spoke with pride of the growth in their children's self-confidence, their ability to use knowledge effectively to resolve public issues, and to stand up for their convictions. Similarly, their teachers saw as most significant students' growth in self-concept. They were proud that these 10 and 11-year-olds were more assertive and confident in speaking to mayor and council, and felt some responsibility for doing something to make their community a better place to live. Videotapes of students being interviewed on TV talk shows and of making their presentation to council support the perceptions of parents and teachers. Students quickly got over initial nervousness and drew on their extensive knowledge of the issue to speak with confidence and persuasion to the adult élite of their community.

Growth in their sense of ethics was also reflected in the conviction with which they supported their decisions. Significantly, students split into three groups, supporting either increased use of chemical spray, use of predators of mosquito larvae, or neither one. The competing social values tied to these alternatives demanded growth in each child's personal belief system, a goal seldom stated or achieved in traditional knowledge and skill dominated curriculum subjects, but central to democratic conceptions of the good person and the good society.

4. Learning from Concrete Experiences

Goodlad described traditional teaching as heavily dependent on lecture and reading textbooks, while audiovisual aids, field trips, guest lecturers, drama, role play, and hands on manipulation of materials "are rarely used as accompaniments or alternatives to textbooks and workbooks as media of instruction" (p. 124). The consequence is that the richness of concrete experiences needed for students to construct personally meaningful knowledge is replaced by more abstract verbal learning. Dale's 'Cone of Experience' (1969) makes the argument that meaningful learning grows from an intake of concrete perceptions from all senses at initial stages of learning, enabling later stages of more abstract conceptual thinking using verbal symbols.

Dale's theory suggests that the base of the cone must provide active, concrete experiences from which can emerge more abstract verbal learning at later stages. Goodlad suggests that the norm is for teachers to ignore the concrete base and begin with verbal abstractions in lecture and textbook form.

The Red Deer project, however, drew heavily on direct experience. Students didn't just read about local government, but had Dale's "direct purposeful experience" with it. They collected pond water and mosquito larvae and used smell, vision, and hearing to learn what happened when predators were introduced into the aquarium. They used role play to experience a simulation of a city council meeting before directly experiencing the real thing. They saw films to learn about use of chemical sprays. They experienced interviews in TV studios to learn about media. Perhaps it is significant that when students went to city council to 'teach' about their preferred solution, one group used a demonstration of predators introduced into an aquarium full of mosquito larvae and another prepared a slide-tape. They in turn used direct concrete experience to begin building understanding.

5. Higher Intellectual Processes

Goodlad criticized traditional schooling for a very heavy emphasis on the lower intellectual processes with "repetitive attention to basic facts and skills" (p. 236). He concluded that schools did not appear to be achieving intellectual development of the ability to think rationally, use, evaluate and accumulate knowledge, understand the implications of knowledge, and either apply it or explore its possible applications. "Only *rarely* did we find evidence to suggest instruction likely to go beyond mere possession of information" (p. 236).

Yet, it was precisely the higher levels of intellectual development Goodlad listed which were dominant in the Red Deer project. Because students heard from partisans of alternative solutions, they were forced to evaluate evidence claims, to detect bias and note how point of view affected interpretations of knowledge. Because they needed to choose an alternative before the city council meeting, they had to organize their knowledge around the competing alternatives, weigh the importance of that knowledge, trace out the implications for them personally, for their community, and for the broader ecosystem and planet of which their community was a part. Their presentations to council demanded the logical organization of their knowledge into a persuasive argument, where their ability to *apply* their knowledge was of overriding importance, while the knowing of the basic facts was merely a first step in the intellectual process.

One hears echoes of Bloom's taxonomy in Goodlad's critique, and in the failure of schools to move beyond the lowest levels of knowing. The Red Deer students progressed to the highest intellectual level of evaluation, in contrast. The focus on an issue to be resolved and acted upon seems to explain the success of the Red Deer project to achieve higher levels of intellectual activity. The need to organize data around alternatives, synthesize data from varied sources, use data to predict future consequences, evaluate the validity of knowledge claims, trace out the implications of economic and environmental data for their futures were all higher levels of intellectual functioning demanded by the need to resolve and act on a contentious social issue with no clear right answer. The teachers' initial decision to set the focus on such an issue planted the seeds for the later use of higher level intellectual operations. Selecting a topic such as "the food chain" or "local government" could have enabled more traditional accumulation of factual knowledge without the mental challenges or growth following from the focus on an issue.

6. Active vs. Passive Citizen

Goodlad was aware of the power of the daily routines teachers followed to shape students' self-perceptions and learned roles. This hidden curriculum constituted what Goodlad typified as "a great hypocrisy" between the school's professed goals of individual flexibility, originality, and creativity and "classroom environments that condition them in precisely opposite behaviors — seeking "right" answers, conforming, and reproducing the known" (p. 241). The hidden curriculum is so powerful because of the daily repetition used to socialize students into "appropriate" roles. These "virtues" are developed by: "The dominant role of the teacher, limited opportunity for student-initiated activity, and quiet passivity of the class group" (p. 241). The teacher dominance and emphasis on knowing the right answers mean that, "One learns passivity. Students in schools are socialized into it virtually from the beginning" (p. 233). Report cards may have a category labeled "Citizenship" implying virtues are obedience to teacher-established rules, passivity, conformity, and respect for authority.

Another element in the image of good citizen results from the emphasis on learning and storing away knowledge rather than using knowledge to try to influence decisions in the community. The good citizen seems to be a consumer of knowledge as Freire's "banking" model of teaching noted (1972). Those who are experts in a subject (teachers or textbook authors) are to be respected, and their knowledge passively received, rather than the student being seen as capable of actively constructing personal knowledge. Such personal knowledge could be applied to resolving and acting on issues confronting the citizens in the community. In Goodlad's schools, the good citizen would appear to be a knowledgeable voter, but not an active participant in advocacy groups trying to make their town a better place to live. The model of good person and good society in Goodlad's schools suggests passive knowing rather than the Red Deer model of active, informed doing. Both models reflect teacher ideology, one knowing about and conserving the existing culture and the other fostering citizens who use their knowledge and convictions to actively work to transform their society toward their ideals. The roles and experiences teachers choose for their students constitute powerful forms of socializing students into preferred good citizen and good person models, and have potential for helping shape alternative models of good society. Acknowledging the sociopolitical role of schooling places a moral responsibility on teachers as they choose their hidden curriculum and implicit ideals of good citizen and good society.

Summary And Questions For Reflection

The Red Deer mosquito project differed markedly from schooling as portrayed by Goodlad in a number of important ways. First, Goodlad argued that traditional schooling holds very little personal relevance for students, that teachers fail to connect the science or math taught to the real life concerns and experiences of their students. The Red Deer project used a local issue of personal significance to students to achieve high levels of personal and social relevance.

Second, Goodlad describes separate subject teaching as artificially segmented rather than integrated around realistic problems. The Red Deer project drew on knowledge and skills which were useful in understanding and acting on their issue, and offered a pragmatic legitimation of knowledge regardless of discipline boundaries.

Third, Goodlad saw schools as narrowly focusing on knowledge goals to the exclusion of social, civic, cultural and personal development. The whole child was being ignored in order to pile up knowledge. The Red Deer project provided opportunities for the whole child to develop in altruism, morality, civic responsibility and personal self-confidence.

Fourth, Goodlad noted the textbook and lecture dominance in teaching, using verbally abstract and passive teaching methods. In contrast, the Red Deer teachers used a wealth of concrete materials and direct experiences to help students use multisensory learning to construct rich, personal meanings.

Fifth, while Goodlad's schools had heavily emphasized lower intellectual processes of memorizing right answers and given facts, the use of inquiry into a local issue leading to social action in Red Deer had engaged students in many activities requiring analysis, synthesis, evaluation, prediction tracing logical implications, and other advanced levels of intellectual operations.

Sixth, Goodlad concluded the hidden curriculum in his schools was to socialize students into passivity and conformity. By emphasizing that students should take social action on their decisions, the Red Deer project nurtured active citizenship and encouraged self-concepts as doers who can successfully act to make their community a better place to live. These teacher choices of passive or active citizenship are moral choices reflecting personal ideology and beliefs about the good person and good society.

These critiques of traditional schooling raise numerous questions about appropriate goals for schooling, teachers' moral responsibility to consciously choose a hidden curriculum which socializes children into either active or passive citizenship, choice of materials and experiences for meaningful learning.

Questions For Critical Reflection

Some of the questions the Red Deer project may help us critically reflect upon include:

1. How can topics or issues be chosen to maximize students' seeing the personal and social relevance of their studies?

2. What are the advantages and disadvantages of using separate subjects and their textbooks and workbooks rather than integrated topics and issues with a wide variety of non-textbook resources?

3. What other kinds of growth besides basic knowledge are important for me to work toward? How would I justify those to parents and principal? What is my ideal "good person?"

4. What is the desirable balance between received knowledge (as from textbooks) and personally constructed knowledge drawn from varied experiences and concrete materials? What are the implications of Dale's Cone of Experience for the selection of materials?

5. How is use of lower intellectual levels and emphasis on "right answers" related to the empowering of teachers? What risks then follow for teachers who emphasize activities requiring critical, creative, and evaluative thinking?

6. What was the nature of your teachers' hidden curriculum? What does that reflect about their ideology or their beliefs about good citizens, good persons, and good societies? What are your own moral beliefs about these issues?

For further information on the Red Deer project, contact: Rick Moore or Don Taylor, Red Deer School District #104, 4147-53 Street, Red Deer, Alberta CANADA

FOOTNOTE
1. These indented sections are taken from Taylor and Moore (1983–4).

References and Related Readings
Bloom, B. (Ed.) (1956). *Taxonomy of educational objectives.* Handbook I: cognitive domain. New York: McKay.

Dale, Edgar (1969). *Audiovisual methods in teaching.* New York: Dryden Press.

Freire, Paulo (1972). *Pedagogy of the oppressed.* New York: Herder & Herder.

Hungerford, H. (1978). *Investigation and action skills for environmental problem solving.* Champaign, Ill.: Stipes Publications Company.

Taylor, Don & Moore, Rick (1983-84). "Red Deer environmental action project," *One World, 12*(2), pp. 8–13.

Chapter Five

Freinet Pedagogy, An Alternative Approach[†]

William B. Lee

Context

If there is a single anecdote known about French education it is
the one about Napoleon's Minister of Education who could, at
11 o'clock on any given day, look at his watch and know precisely what French school children would be studying. The story
is probably apocryphal but it does introduce one of the distin-
guishing aspects of French education, its centralization. Today it
is still true that most of the important educational decisions are
made in Paris even though in recent years many educational
responsibilities have been delegated to the "Academies," an
administration division of which there are 26 in France; however there is still a national curriculum and the national inspectors
who control the curriculum and supervise and evaluate the
teachers. This contrasts sharply to the historical development of
schools in North America where important curricular and per-
sonnel decisions have been made locally even though today this
is changing somewhat as the states and provinces are providing
more and more of the needed funding and the unwanted control

[†] This chapter previously appeared in *Canadian Social Studies*, 27(4), 1993,
pp. 146–151.

that goes with it. Despite recent tendencies on both sides of the Atlantic, from the perspective of North Americans French education is still highly centralized.

A second aspect of French education is its traditional orientation. The nine patterns of teaching and learning that Goodlad found so pervasive in American schools would not have surprised the average French person at all. If such a study were ever to be conducted in France one would wonder why, when the findings would be so predictable. The difference here is that the results surprised and disappointed Goodlad and his fellow researchers. Central to both Goodlad's and Cuban's research is the assumption that education should be child-centered and that assumption is simply lacking in French schools. Implicit in Goodlad's study is that traditional education is bad and must be changed to child-centered. Not so in France.

Let us envision how an imaginary French critic might respond to the nine pervasive patterns cited by Goodlad in the introductory chapter as they apply to French schools. The exaggerations if any, are only slight.

Patterns 1, 3 and 4 describe the dominant role of the teacher. This is as it should be. Teachers are educated and trained to impart the *culture generale* to the children.

Patterns 6 and& 7 cite the lack of variety in the teaching methodology. But please remember that teachers are not there to entertain students but rather to instruct them. If they want to be entertained they should go to a movie. School is a place of hard work and not necessarily to be enjoyed.

Patterns 2, 8 and 9 describe respectively: students working alone rather than together, their passivity, and the fact that they often did not understand or finish work. The rationale for students working together is puzzling. There is the danger of their exchanging erroneous information and after all examinations are taken individually and not collectively. As for their passivity what exactly is the relationship between activity and the acquisition of knowledge? And finally if they did not understand the lesson they probably were not listening carefully and should do so next time. As for not finishing their work, they are to work harder or to take it home to finish it.

As for the hypocrisy cited, it is not only hypocritical but foolhardy when the schools attempt personal, social and cultural goals that they are incapable of achieving. Schools can not be held accountable for such abstract notions as creative self expression, individual flexibility, originality and creativity. These are perhaps desirable traits but beyond the reach of the school and more logically the responsibility of the family, the church, youth and sports organizations. Certainly not the school.

In France there is a broad consensus among teachers and parents as to the intellectual orientation of schools which can be summarized around these four points:

1. Schools are primarily concerned with cognitive learning as opposed to affective, psychomotor and social.

2. A primary goal is the transmission of a body of knowledge that is largely literary and about which there is general although not universal agreement. It is called *culture generale* and tends to be stable with minimal changes from decade to decade.

3. Much learning (education) is good in and of itself and need not have any practical application.

4. Learning about past events is important, either for its own sake or to understand the contemporary world.

The schools in France reflect this intellectual orientation. The seven statements below with brief explanatory remarks describe the overwhelming majority of French schools:

1. School is a place for hard work, not play. Piaget was wrong in saying that play was a child's work. The true analogy is that of the child's father who must go to work whether he finds it enjoyable or not. So with the child.

2. The physical environment of the classroom tends to be sparse and austere although this is certainly less true in the primary grades.

3. The curriculum is divided into separate academic subjects. One does not have language arts, but reading, spelling, grammar and dictation. Not social studies but history and geography.

4. A special emphasis is placed on the 3 Rs: reading, writing

and arithmetic. Feeling good about oneself is not a priority but may be a by-product of being able to read, write and compute.

5. High levels of achievement are expected and high standards are enforced. Currently about half of French elementary school children repeat at least one grade. The lack of praise (Goodlad's pattern #5) could well be appropriate especially if the child is not deserving. If fact praise could well deceive the child and the parent into thinking that she is doing well when she is not.

6. A competitive atmosphere prevails with winners and losers. Until recently schoolchildren were given class rankings, and these were announced to the class each week.

7. Roles are clearly defined:
   • the teacher is to dispense information and to evaluate the pupil's written and oral work.
   • the most common pupil activities are drill, recitation, memorization, analysis and writing.
   • parents play a limited and subordinate role.

The Freinet Classroom: A Personal Note

With this background one hardly expects to see classrooms in France other than those conforming pretty much to the nine patterns described by Goodlad and endorsed by our imaginary French critic. Freinet classrooms are different, but before I describe one for you I would like to tell you about my introduction to them. In the 1960s I and other professors at the University of Southern California had shown the film "Passion for Life" (the French title is *Ecole Buissoniere* or literally playing hookey) in conjunction with the reading of John Dewey's *Experience and Education* (Dewey, 1963). The book contrasts a traditional with a more child-centered approach to education and the film dramatically illustrates these differences. It is about a veteran of World War I who begins his teaching career in the early 1920s in a two-room school in southern France replacing a recently retired teacher who much to his chagrin sees the newcomer introduce a child centered approach to education. He begins by removing the raised platform of the teacher, the symbol of his authority and of the gap between him and his pupils, and breaking it up for firewood. The teacher, now on the same level as the children, is able to move freely among them. His role is transformed from the authoritarian dispenser of knowledge to the guide and the facilitator, and the children, no longer dependent on him, learn to discover knowledge for themselves.

The classroom expands into the village and the nearby fields and forests. The children interview and observe local artisans at work, draw up plans for a new village fountain and build a dam and a small hydroelectric plant on a nearby stream.

Once back in the classroom these "reporters" write about their adventures carefully rewriting and correcting mistakes in grammar and then share these compositions with each other.

Early in the film a dramatic moment occurs. The teacher appears with a mysterious package which after a certain amount of suspense is opened and found to contain printer's type. Now realizing that with a printing press they could share their exploits with others they draw up the plans and a printing press is later built by one of the fathers, a carpenter. Together they select the better compositions which are then compiled into a booklet and sold in the village. Still later, seeking an even wider audience, they exchange these booklets as well as personal and group letters with a class in Brittany in northern France.

The film although situated in France and in the '20s has a timeless quality about it and serves as an excellent springboard for a discussion of the contrasts between a traditional and a more child-centered education. I had assumed it was pure fiction until 1973 when escorting a group of teachers through French schools. As I had been a frequent visitor I was shown a classroom that was different than the others, a Freinet classroom. Much to my astonishment what I saw could well have been taken from the film: desks scattered in small clusters around the room and the teacher moving informally among the children aiding and encouraging them while they were working individually or cooperatively with classmates individual and small group activities. And off in the corner was the printing press with a group of children setting type and preparing to reproduce the compositions that their classmates had written. It was my personal discovery in the real life of the Freinet classroom.

The film, I learned, was based on the life of Celestin Freinet (1896–1966) and portrayed his early efforts to transform his class from being teacher dominated to one that is child centered. He was founder of the movement called the *Ecole Moderne* and currently one finds Freinet classrooms in public schools in all of the 95 French departments. There is also an international section with members in at least 15 other countries most of which are in Europe but also in South America and Africa. It is mainly an elementary school movement but there are teachers who attempt to adapt his pedagogy to junior and senior high school students.

Another remarkable aspect of the Ecole Moderne, the first being of course its very existence within the structure of French education, is the clear continuity of educational principles between those advocated by Freinet and those guiding the movement today, almost seventy years later. This continuity extends to Freinet classrooms themselves. The one described below, attended by my two sons for 2 1/2 years in the early 1980s (adapted and up-dated from Lee, 1983b), resembles those taught by Freinet and his early followers half a century earlier and as well those that you can visit in France in the 1990s.

The Classroom

Even a glance into the room without the children alerts the visitor that this is not an ordinary French classroom. The seating arrangements might be in almost any configuration except in straight rows facing the front and dominated by the teacher's desk and lectern. The tables, stools, desks and chairs are arranged in informal configurations encouraging communication and easy movement among the children. The arrangement may change during the day depending on the individual or cooperative learning activities.

The walls display the life of the class. The children's work overflows from the bulletin board and adorns almost every available space. Artistic endeavours abound: drawings, paintings, and collages, as well as creative written work both prose and poetry — often products of the class printing press and usually handsomely decorated. The more routine aspects of the classroom life are there also, the carefully completed and neatly written homework (in ink of course) serving as an example of how all assignments should look.

Seemingly out of place amidst these creative efforts are large posters illustrating formal lessons of grammar: conjugation of regular and irregular verbs, agreement of subject and verb, and sentences dividing words into groups resembling the little practiced and often discredited American practice of diagramming sentences. Almost all of these words and phrases are taken from the children's work and are reminders to them that effective communication and creative expression must conform to rules of correct usage.

Also exhibited on the classroom wall are individual or committee reports accompanied by postcards, photos, drawings, clippings from newspapers and other forms of documentation. The common denominator of the topics is that they are of interest to the children and often have an impact on their lives and the lives of their families. Some of the topics are visits to the ruins of Roman aqueducts, the local cathedral, the Verdun battlefields, and interviews with the local shoemaker, baker and members of the City Council. (One teacher reported that when the children took notes the council members became nervous.) Also dealt with are current social and economic issues such as unemployment (Christopher's father is out of work. Why?), inadequacy of local parks and playgrounds, pollution, nuclear power, children living in poverty and famine in Africa. Ideally these items of personal interest lead to first hand observations and inquiries and later to additional documentation from newspapers, magazines and books.

Nature is also on display. Living and growing plants and animals are on tables placed against the walls and sometimes jutting into the central classroom space. Some of the plants have been grown from seedlings, others found on a class field trip in nearby forest and fields, while still others may have been found on the way to school that morning. Animal life includes aquariums containing guppies, goldfish and more exotic types of fish, terrariums with lizards, snakes, gerbils and large cages with turtle doves or canaries.

Cooperative

The Cooperative is the nerve centre of the Freinet pedagogy and every classroom has one. It is the organization that reflects and guides the life of the class. It resembles class governments with class officers that one sometimes finds in American schools but is less formal and less competitive relying more on consensus and cooperation. For example rather than being elected, class officers are rotated throughout the school year with each child having the opportunity to serve as president, treasurer or secretary or perhaps all three.

Usually the week begins with a meeting of the cooperative on Monday morning. It resembles the "show and tell" of American schools with the children sharing their weekend activities and responding to the questions of their classmates. The following would be typical dialogue for a second grade class:

'MY SISTER HAD A FEVER"
How high was it? How was it measured?

"I BUILT A MODEL AIRPLANE WITH MY FATHER"
What are its dimensions?
Can you bring it to class?

"WE GOT A NEW DOG"
What is its name?
What does it eat?
Is it house broken?

The teacher serves as facilitator, encouraging the timid to participate, provoking questions when none are asked and gently but firmly correcting errors of language usually by modeling the correct or more accurate response. You can also be certain that he is taking notes mental or written so he can incorporate these items of interest to the children into the more formal lessons of grammar or history.

On Monday morning the periodic rotation of responsibilities takes place. These have been decided upon during a meeting of the cooperative early in the school year and may differ somewhat from class to class but below is a rather typical list:

President
Secretary

Treasurer (2)
Representatives to the school cooperative (2)
caring for the plants and animals (2−4)
checking out books from the library
writing the date on the chalk board
cleaning the chalkboard
storing and returning the backpacks
storing and returning the gym materials
cleaning of table
stacking of stools
distribution of materials for painting
mounting of displays on bulletin boards and walls (2−4)
distributions of letters from "corespondents"
distribution of folders containing classwork.

Once the assignments are made they are posted publicly so that these are known by each child in the class.

The reigning principle is that each child has a responsibility, although in smaller classes it could be more than one and in larger classes it might be shared with a classmate. Some tasks are shared because they are time-consuming such as a class with several cages, aquariums, and terrariums to be tended each day. Others are shared because they are relatively complex. The treasurer is a good example. Three-dollar dues are collected each tri-mester and these may come trickling in over several weeks, stamps must be bought for packages sent to the correspondents (more later), and other expenses approved by Cooperative must be made and accounted for, which nevertheless expects accurate and open books to be kept.

When unexpected needs arise — a package, say, has to be mailed after school — the teacher would probably ask for a volunteer; if participation at a special weekend conference is limited to one or two, the selection would be made by drawing from a box containing the name of each class member on a slip of paper.

It is during the meeting of the Cooperative that the everyday problems of classroom living are discussed. Is the classroom too noisy? Are some children interfering with the work of others? Are class responsibilities (plants watered, fish fed, cages cleaned) being carried out? Should seating assignments be changed? Is the arrangement of tables and desks satisfactory?

Who will take the animals home over the vacation? One of the hamsters has died and another class has babies to sell. Renaud is in the hospital. Shall we send him a card?

School problems are also aired. Do the older children have a preferred part of the playground? Are they ganging up on the younger children? Are the school hallways cluttered or dirty? Which class is responsible? Are the chickens, doves and rabbits in the large cage in the courtyard being properly fed? Do other classes use the multi-purpose room more than we do? When is the next meeting of the school Cooperative? What items do we want on the agenda?

These issues are dealt with in a variety of ways. Sometimes reminding the class of an existing class rule (low level of noise) may resolve the problem; if not, an informal reminder to the offender usually does. In case of repeated violations, the teacher usually heads off overly punitive action by discussing the situation with the offender before the next meeting of the Cooperative. As a last resort parents may be informed and a conference arranged. Some issues can not be resolved immediately without additional information (how much will the baby hamster cost?), or without consulting with others (taking animals home for the weekend) and still others call for further discussions among members of the class (agenda items for the school Cooperative). Of course not all problems can be resolved to the satisfaction of the class (use of the multi-purpose room) or may not even be resolvable (incompatibility among classmates) but an open discussion somehow makes them more palatable than before.

In these deliberations the teacher plays a more direct role than in the earlier part of the meeting. He as the more mature member of the group is clearly the "leader of group activities" in John Dewey's terms (Dewey, 1963, p. 53). He moderates potentially harsh decisions, moves from one topic to another when further discussion seems useless, provides information that the children could not possibly be aware of (school policy and scheduling of the multi-purpose room), suggests postponement when the need of additional information is obvious, and skillfully guides the group toward consensual decision making whenever possible.

The Cooperative facilitates personalized instruction by

enabling the teacher to observe the child in a variety of circumstances: telling about his personal and family life in class meetings, carrying out his assigned responsibilities, reacting to suggestions and criticisms, and in carrying out the leadership role of class president, an office that is rotated and not reserved for the most popular or even the most capable child. The Cooperative also makes more time available for personalized instruction by relieving the teacher of many of the routine, time-consuming classroom chores. This arrangement also develops the child's self-reliance and autonomy traits which it is hoped will carry over to the child's academic work and personal life.

In the Freinet classroom the community is an extension of the classroom. It is a two way street with children going out into the community and its members coming into the school. During the school day children visit nearby museums and historical sites, attend theatrical and musical events and are shown how local farms and businesses operate. Often these visits require follow-up inquiries and interviews with local officials, scholars, artists, artisans and business people. Parents feel free to drop in before and after school for an informal conference with the teacher and are encouraged to observe a portion of the class itself. They also are often utilized as tutors.

Much of what has been described is, of course, the antithesis of traditional education and contrary to the nine patterns that Goodlad found in American schools:

- education begins with everyday events in the lives of children
- the children make meaningful decisions about their learning
- the teacher guides not dominates the instructional process
- there are a variety of classroom activities
- most of the activities are collaborative not competitive

However the Freinet pedagogy is interspersed with traditional elements: conjugating of verbs, diagramming of sentences, the insistence on high standards, and that schoolwork be completed neatly and correctly (sloppy work is just not accepted), and the emphasis on the 3 Rs. How can this be explained? By taking into account the historical and social context. Most Freinet educators agree with their inclusion, viewing these elements as part of education and neither traditional nor child-centered. Also any hint that these traditional aspects be discarded would meet with fierce resistance from the general public and from the parents of the children themselves. Another more practical factor is that the Freinet classroom is part of the public school system and all of the elementary school children will eventually attend traditional public schools. One cannot claim to be really "child-centered" and yet set the youngster up for future failure by neglecting to teach skills and knowledge to survive in a rigorous academic curriculum at the secondary level.

Societal expectations for schooling are best illustrated in the question parents ask when the child returns home: "As-tu bien travaille?" Did you work well in school? "What happened?" or "Did you enjoy yourself?" or least of all "Did you have fun?" Schoolwork may at times be rewarding and fulfilling, but it is most of all hard work.

The Freinet educator is set apart from the traditional educator in the belief that this hard work can be accomplished with the child actively participating in his or her own learning in an orderly, disciplined classroom without the teacher dominating the organization of the class and being the sole, authoritative source of information.

Tools And Techniques

Freinet's early teaching experiences with his own class convinced him of the necessity of developing techniques and materials for child-centered teaching. He recalled that after an exhilarating *classe promenade* into the nearby countryside and an animated discussion of it in class, he, for the lack of adequate tools and techniques, returned to traditional methodology (the teacher talking) and traditional content (the textbook). Freinet attached the highest priority and an extraordinary sense of urgency to developing materials to assist teachers who were floundering, like he was, in ordinary classrooms like his own.

Granted that new materials were necessary but who should develop them? For Freinet the answer is easy — the teachers themselves. It is they who have daily contact with the children, and they who know the children best. The teacher, as artisan, is especially neddful of complex tools, because his raw material — the child — is especially complex.

> We are not theorists, but practitioners. Practitioners who like other artisans at their work benches, sometimes with limited theoretical knowledge, invent and perfect their tools, devise special processes, techniques of the trade that they manage later to systemize in order to offer them [tools and techniques] to their colleagues.... (Freinet, 1969, p. 72)

The French word used by members of the *Ecole Moderne* is *outil* which in the broad sense means any technique, strategy or materials that the teacher uses. The Cooperative that we described earlier is an *outil*. Privileged in the Freinet repertoire is the printing press first introduced by Freinet in 1924 and used in my sons' classes in the 1980s but now in all except the very early grades is being replaced by E-mail and Faxes (more later).

The latest catalogue of the *Ecole Moderne* contains almost fifty pages of teacher-made materials: individualized task cards (resembling SRA kits in all subjects but especially math and reading), periodicals for several age groups, audio-tapes and slide multi-media presentations, eight pages of programmed instructional materials in math and French and several pedagogical booklets for teachers written by Freinet himself. Each of the last 10 pages contains a description of one of the 10 periodicals published by the *Publications de l'Ecole Moderne Francaise* (PEMF) with the specific age groups for which they are intended. (More about these later.)

In some ways the Freinet classroom resembles a child-centered classroom in North America, even the ones described by Goodlad in the primary grades (Goodlad, p. 227). However, there is no American counterpart to the *Ecole Moderne* and the success of teachers themselves in developing classroom techniques and materials to make child-centered teaching possible.

Cooperation

One of the guiding principles permeating Freinet pedagogy is cooperation. This is illustrated by the class and school Cooperatives described earlier. But teachers also work together cooperatively in monthly meetings of departmental groups, in national commissions and in national and international congresses. Like so much of the movement these meetings bear the imprint of Freinet who initiated them in the '20s not only to exchange professional information but also establish a sort of esprit de corps among child-centered educators who at their schools may feel isolated among more traditional teachers.

It is at these meetings, or through their professional journal *le nouvel educateur*, that they make arrangements with their sister classes, their *correspondents*. Each Freinet class has one or more class with whom they communicate regularly by exchanging individual letters, class letters, and packets containing compositions, poetry and drawings. This sister class may be nearby, so that personal visits are easier, or in another part of France, so that the children can learn about a new and different area. (Freinet initiated these in 1924 with a class in Brittany about 1,000 kilometres from his school in southern France.) The *correspondents* of my sons' classes were in the Vosges mountains which we, children, teachers and chaperones, visited in the winter during ski season and in turn were hosts to them during the spring, when we arranged, among other activities, a visit to the battlefields of Verdun. The personal and social benefits are obvious but another tangible one is the wider audience, which provides another outlet for their creative efforts and for their written work. (Remember, it must be neat and correct to be understood!)

Technological developments have expanded communication among Freinet classrooms. The traditional exchanges of children's letters and creative work now includes video tapes but even more dramatic is the use of E-mail and FAX. One Freinet class receives between 10 and 30 E-mail messages daily. These are sorted and recorded by the children, the most urgent of which are discussed in the meeting of Cooperative. FAX messages are handled similarly but usually receive more immediate responses.

This may appear to be a revolutionary transformation of a Freinet classroom but it really is not. Freinet pedagogy has easily absorbed the new technology because communication has always been emphasized and is such a necessary part of cooperation. One Freinet teacher summarizes it this way. "We use the tools of communication because we communicate. We do not communicate because we *have* the tools of communication" (Beaumont, 1992, emphasis mine). Only on the surface is the class of the '90s different than the one taught by Freinet in the '20s or the one attended by my sons in the '80s.

The materials in the catalogue mentioned earlier are one of the results of cooperative, teacher efforts. These are conceived, designed and tried out in Freinet classrooms and are later produced and distributed by the successor to the cooperative founded by Freinet in 1926 (PEMF, 1992).

One of the ten periodicals is the *Biblioteque de Travail Junior* (BTJ) for 9 to 11-year-olds which appears 12 times a year and whose recent issues have included such diverse topics as The Sun in the Universe, Lizards, Dinosaurs, Recycling, and the Future of Electric Cars. Also questions about personal problems of this age group are included: How to make purchases wisely? Where do babies come from? and What causes wetting the bed?

The starting point for these periodicals is the classroom. A teacher and her children may have had a particularly successful unit on one of these topics and wish to share it with others. A first draft is prepared and tried out by other teachers with their classes. They in turn make recommendations for improvement until when it is ready for publication it is submitted to a national teacher committee of the *Ecole Moderne* for possible revisions. Children are an integral part of this process and are listed as co-authors. Also acknowledged are the collaborating teachers and their classes and any expert who may have been consulted.

In North American schools one can find examples of teachers working together cooperatively, student exchanges and teacher-student efforts, but the Freinet movement is unique in having a well established infrastructure to assist teachers in initiating such action and in sustaining their efforts.

Child-Centered Activism

Freinet educators see a logical connection between a child-centered classroom and a general advocacy of the child beyond the boundaries of the school. If hunger, racism and inadequate housing interfere with a child learning in school, do not the same conditions also affect the child after school hours? One can not be truly child-centered and still ignore the out-of-school problems of the child.

Even though most Freinet educators would agree with this extension of child-centred learning, there are, nevertheless two large, distinctive groups within the *Ecole Moderne* with different priorities: the *Politiques* and the *Pedagogues*. The *Pedagogues*, as the name implies, are primarily interested in classroom and curricular matters. Most would want to humanize and democratize the class and most likely are attracted to the movement because of dissatisfaction with their own teaching, which they hope to improve with the tools and techniques of the *Ecole Moderne*. In political terms these pedagogues could be relatively conservative and believe that the child is best served by teaching him or her how to read and write and that the injustices within society should be handled through existing institutions.

The *Politiques* are attracted to the movement because of its recognition that social and economic issues, racism and poverty, have an impact on the child either directly or through their families. Confronting and attempting to resolve these issues, they believe is more urgent than a new technique to teach reading and French. (For a more complete account see Lee, 1983a.)

A recent front page editorial in *le nouvel educateur*, the professional journal of the movement, represents this point of view. The authors call attention to the rise of racism in France and the increased number of the population who think that all immigrants should go home. They are alarmed when racist statements by reputable politicians result in a sharp rise in their personal popularity. They plead with the *pedagogues* to look beyond the comfort of their class and of their Cooperative and to confront these urgent social issues (Laurent-Fahier and Debarbieux, 1992).

These two tendencies within a single organization are of course potentially divisive and have been since the 1920's. But one must remember that they, compared to the traditional educators, have much that binds them together: respect for the child, two way communication, the many cooperative activities, the variety of teaching techniques and the democratic participation in organizing the class. Their common ground, the child-centered classroom, is viewed differently by the two groups. For the *pedagogue* it is often justified by an uncomplicated respect for and faith in the child, while the *politique* sees it as a political statement, a radical act of defiance to allow children to have a voice in their own affairs in school when they and their parents have so little control of their own lives within the existing, oppressive society.

Freinet and his contemporary followers would agree that teaching is a moral act rather than a technical decision based on doing things faster and better (Tom, 1984), but would add that teachers are also morally obligated to confront the social injustices in society affecting the child directly or indirectly or through the intermediary of the family. "Pedagogically speaking, we do not have the right to ignore the errors and injustices [of society] which affect the child beyond our [the schools] supervision and responsibility" (Freinet, 1969, p. 25). Freinet's advice, still followed today, is that teachers must take an active role in child advocacy issues but leaves the type of involvement up to the individual teacher's philosophical, religious and political orientation. How one will become involved is a personal decision; whether one should be, is not.

I am often asked how such a child-centered and politically active educational movement manages to exist within the centralized and traditional French educational system. The answer as I understand it is as follows. Within the French context centralization does not mean less freedom but probably more. Paris is a great distance from most schools both geographically and bureaucratically. Directives must travel through multiple layers of bureaucracy to schools where the teacher is to implement them and where sometimes the essence or even the substance is lost in transit. (A commission of the Association of Teachers of History and Geography recently met to evaluate the first year of the new program and some of the teachers were unaware of its existence [Lee, 1992].) Centralization also protects the teacher from local interferences because everyone knows that the major decisions are made in Paris. It is there, rather than the local school, where pressure must be brought to bear. It is futile to attempt to initiate change locally.

In a curious way, the traditional, subject matter orientation also increases a teacher's freedom. The local administrator is not thought competent to evaluate all grade levels and all disciplines so this is done by a special inspectoral corps at the level of the department or the *Academie* and only infrequently (every three or four years). Sometimes these Inspectors, especially at the primary level, are even sympathetic to Freinet pedagogy and support rather than inhibit a teacher's effort to individualize and humanize instruction.

In North America centralization is equated with loss of freedom but this is clearly not true in France. And after all one may ask why should control that is far away be more inhibiting than control that is nearby?

Summary And Conclusions

Freinet pedagogy because of its long history, its mixture of child-centered and traditional elements, its elevation of the role of the teacher and its insistence on a child-centered activism provides an especially rich perspective from which to critique traditional education as well as the findings of Goodlad and Cuban. Below are some of the issues that are raised.

1. Can children learn the necessary fundamentals in a child-centered classroom?

2. Does a child-centered pedagogy prepare a child for later life when he or she will have little say in decisions that affect his or her own life, i.e. working in large bureaucratic organizations?

3. Are carrying out classroom responsibilities taking away time that children should spend on academic subjects?

4. At what age can a child make important decisions about his or her learning?

5. Is the role of the teacher diminished by permitting children to carry out teacher responsibilities?

6. In France and in Freinet pedagogy it is believed that work is more fundamental than play. What do you think?

7. If child-centered pedagogy can exist and even thrive within a very traditional French system, why did Goodlad find so little evidence of it in a less traditional North American system?

8. Is it possible to have a child-centered pedagogy without a stable support group such as the *Ecole Moderne*?

9. Is "the teacher as artisan" an apt analogy?

10. Can one be child-centered and still ignore social issues such as poverty, racism and unemployment that affect the child either directly or through the family?

11. What is the moral obligation of teachers and who decides?

12. In North America teachers are thought to be incapable of developing their own curricular materials and we rely on "experts" such as psychologists, curriculum consultants and university professors. Yet, Freinet pedagogy relies on teacher-made materials. How can this be explained?

13. Perhaps the assumption that centralization decreases freedom should be re-examined in view of the example of France. Do local rather then national pressures have the most impact on schools in North America?

Further information about Freinet pedagogy: For a catalogue see the address in the references. To participate in electronic exchanges contact: Alex Lafosse, Le Roc Bediere, 24200 Sarlat, France

To know more about the international section contact: Birgitta Kovermann, W. Leuscher, Str. 6 B Reklinhausen, Germany

References

Beaumont, R. (1992, janvier). "La classe, structure de la communication," *le nouvel educateur*, pp. 1–2.

Dewey, J. (1963). *Experience and Education.* New York: Collier Books.

Freinet, C. (1969). *Pour l'ecole du peuple* (combines two previously published books *Ecole moderne francaise*, 1943 and *Invariants pedagogiques*, 1964). Paris: Francois Maspero.

Laurent-Fahier, A. & Debarbieux, E. (1992, janvier). "Racisme: Le devoir de s'engager," *le nounvel educateur*, pp. 1, 3.

Lee, W. (1983a). "The child centered radicalism of the ecole moderne," *Journal of Abstracts in International Education*, *12*(1), 7–27.

Lee, William B. (1983b). "Classrooms of the ecole moderne." in *Philosophy of Education, Proceedings, 1983*. Earl Grossen (Ed.). Provo, Utah: Brigham Young University Publications.

Lee, W. (1992). "History during the French lycee terminale year: An unexpected reform," *The History Teacher*, *25*(2), 193–189.

Publications de l'Ecole Moderne Francaise (1992). *General Catalogue 92–93* (Available from Publications de l'Ecole Moderne Francaise, 06376 Mouans-Sartoux Cedex, France.)

See also *Cooperative Learning and Social Change: Selected Writings of Célestin Freinet*, edited and translated by David Clandfield and John Sivell, Our Schools/Our Selves, Toronto, 1990.

Chapter Six

Waldorf (Steiner) Schools

Karl-Georg Ahlström

Kristoffer School — A Swedish Waldorf School

Its very exterior announces that Kristoffer School — the oldest and largest Waldorf school in Sweden — is a different kind of school. Arrayed in a semicircle from the large angular central building looming over other buildings atop a cliff in a Stockholm suburb there are a number of one-story buildings of various sizes, heights, and colours. The roofs describe different angles and are often truncated, but never symmetrical and identical. The colours, too, differ from those usually used for Swedish buildings. Some people dislike the asymmetry and colouring, all the more since the whole complex seems to have been designed this way. Others are beguiled by the bold shapes and "abnormal" colour spectrum.

In the classrooms the desks are placed in the form of a horseshoe, with a large desk for the teacher in the opening of the horseshoe. In contrast with the public schools, where there are never more than 25 and often a maximum of 20 pupils in a class, there are rarely fewer than 30 students in Kristoffer School classes. The desks are often old-fashioned and not always of the same model, but they are in good condition and well kept. The rest of the equipment also strikes one as meager. For instance, there are no overhead projectors, which have been standard issue in all Swedish schoolrooms for decades. Nor are there slide projectors, video monitors, tape recorders, or central radios. The paintings and sculptures that adorn the walls are generally the work of students. The ceiling lamps are a simple but practical construction of wood and cloth, and they provide "soft" lighting. There are masses of flowers in all windows. It can hardly be for purely economic reasons that "normal" teaching aids are absent, because the furniture and textiles in the lounges are of high quality.

Both the outer and inner forms of the equipment indicate that this is a school with a specific pedagogical philosophy. Of course, most Waldorf schools have not had the same economic latitude as Kristoffer School when it comes to manifesting this philosophy in a certain architectural form and interior design, but rather have had to carry out their teaching in whatever buildings have happened to be available. Nonetheless, all Waldorf schools do share the same educational program, that is the objectives, organization, and content of the teaching. This is what we will focus on below, attempting to show at the same time how the school's appearance and interior decoration are linked to the content of its activities, and how form and content can be derived from the theoretical underpinnings of Waldorf pedagogy. First a few words about the origin and dissemination of that pedagogy.

The Origin And Dissemination
Of Waldorf Pedagogy

At the suggestion of the workers at the Waldorf Astoria cigarette factory in Stuttgart, Rudolf Steiner was asked by the factory's progressive management to start a school for the employees' children. Steiner's ideas had gained their confidence after he had delivered a series of speeches about the possibility of improving the workers' lot through general education.

In 1919, when this happened, Steiner was 58 years old and had led a varied life. He was a trained engineer but had evinced a strong interest in philosophy even in his college days. From the age of 14 he had financed his studies by working as a private tutor. As regards the pedagogical ideas he would later develop, he ascribes particular importance to his experiences with a boy who was so severely handicapped by hydrocephalus as to be considered "uneducable" when he came under Steiner's tutelage at the age of ten. Despite this fact, the boy managed to finish both elementary and high school, and eventually, with Steiner's help, was even able to go to medical school and become a doctor.

Since he had such extensive knowledge of both science and philosophy, Steiner was asked at a tender age to help with an edition of Goethe's scientific writings. His own thinking subsequently came to be clearly colored by Goethe's ideas. After finishing his doctor's degree in philosophy, he worked for a few years as the editor of a cultural journal and later as a teacher at the school for the education of workers in Berlin. In parallel with this he wrote a series of books and magazine articles and lectured on various themes of philosophy, religion, and social criticism. He was soon drawn to theosophy, which is strongly influenced by Indian philosophy, but after having been secretary general of the German branch of the Theosophical Society, he broke with the theosophists and started the Anthroposophic Society in 1912.

Like theosophy, anthroposophy does not wish to be a set system of thought, replete with dogmas to be accepted in good faith. In contrast with a religion, the philosophy sees itself as an empirical, scientific road to knowledge of the world, of humankind, and of the self. The method for attaining such knowledge is reflection and meditation based on strict self-discipline and schooling.

The *fundamentals* of these theories have been adopted by the members of the movement. But, as mentioned above, anthroposophy is not a set system; on the contrary, its pedagogy, for example, is undergoing constant development, assuming local variants, though all of these derive from the cardinal ideas that Steiner developed in his writings.

When the movement was banned in Germany in 1935, it spread — not least its schools — all over the world. With the possible exception of Asia, the anthroposophists' Waldorf schools and medicopedagogical institutes are now active in all parts of the globe (including the former eastern European block). Their teachers' training exists in England, Holland, Switzerland, Sweden, Germany and the United States. A meeting place for members is the Goetheanum, which is the anthroposophists' college in Dornach, Switzerland.

Some Methodological Principles Of Waldorf Pedagogy

Let us now visit a class and take part in some lessons. Why not a seventh-grade class? The morning session is just getting underway.

Taking Into Consideration Diurnal Rhythm

The day always starts with two periods without a break, two lessons involving knowledge acquisition. It is thought to be easier to absorb new experiences and thoughts in the mornings. This is normally followed by language instruction, the teacher tells us: "It's not merely a matter of apprehending pictures and thoughts but primarily of developing a feeling for the language and constantly practicing what you have already learned." Language can alternate with music, among other subjects. The last couple of hours of the school day — when exhaustion usually sets in — are mainly devoted to practicing skills, such as calculating and writing, and to pursuits in arts and crafts plus, in the upper grades, labs, geometric construction, map-making, and the like. So every school day has a rhythm that might be characterized by the motto: from experience to action.

The theories of Waldorf pedagogy contain certain conceptions of what the daily rhythm of humans is like and stress the importance of taking this into consideration when planning the school day. Generally speaking the curriculum and therefore the content and organization of the school are firmly anchored in Steiner's thinking about psychological development.

Periodic Studies

In periods of three to four weeks the morning hours of each day are devoted to one and the same knowledge-based subject — the native language, mathematics, history, geography, etc., and a certain theme is treated thoroughly. By working continuously with one and the same theme, the pupils do not risk losing the broad view by dividing their attention because of other projects. The possibility of penetrating the subject in depth is also enhanced, according to the teacher. "The period" is always rounded off with some sort of report about what has been accomplished. After that it may be quite some time before that particular subject returns, perhaps a full term or even longer. Waldorf teachers feel that it does not matter if the students forget the details of their work in the interim. What matters is the perspective they acquired and their understanding of contexts.

The instruction offered during a period is characterized, on the one hand, by oral presentation, which the teacher provides, and, on the other hand, by "period booklets," which the students produce on the basis of the teacher's presentation. There are no traditional textbooks whatsoever in the school.

The teacher presents the content of the theme as vividly and interestingly as possible, illustrating the talk with drawings on the blackboard, with pictures from books and magazines, with sections read aloud from books, and with episodes experienced by either the whole group, part of the group, or individual pupils and that relate to the theme. Of course, the teacher also tries to inspire the students to ask questions. Questions and the teacher's and other students' comments on them also help to make the content concrete and to create variety in the lesson. Pupils can be asked to try to find complementary information in books at the library in their spare time, but the content of the theme is mediated by the teacher.

The students normally recreate what the teacher has told them in their "period booklets," a report book that can comprise a dozen pages and which is provided with a decorative cover displaying the title of the theme. In the lower grades the teacher dictates the main features of the presentation, though leaving scope for the pupils to add whatever complementary information they might wish, perhaps a picture or two, or an episode they have talked about. Gradually, in the upper grades, the students are given ever greater responsibility for the selection of content and choice of form for the presentation. Some students want to treat certain aspects of a theme more exhaustively and in greater detail than other aspects; other students perhaps prefer to construct their report around pictures with complementary texts, producing report booklets that resemble comic books. They are free to do so. What is important is that each student should take up central aspects of the theme.

In our class the theme is the French Revolution, which they have nearly finished. The teacher had suggested that they not report on the work in the form of period booklets. Instead, each and every pupil was to write an essay during the last few hours, and what's more the class was to work on a production of a play about the revolution that the teacher had written together with a colleague. There were a dozen essay topics, for example, a speech made before the Jacobin Club in September 1792, some thoughts about the Declaration of Human Rights, one of the key figures of the revolution, etc. The students had two aids: a list of important events and a copy of the declaration. The play is to be performed in the evening two weeks later in the assembly hall before the whole school. The students have now chosen what roles they want to play; some have chosen to work with the curtain and stage props during the play. Some students have built some of the props in their wood shop class. They have chosen a few French songs, including the Marseillaise, and practiced them during their music lessons. The students have sought help with what their costumes should look like by looking in reference books, and during their textile shop class they have altered old clothes to make them fit the epoch.

During the classes we are visiting, the teacher returns the essays, corrected and supplied with comments like: "a very interesting point, but couldn't you have taken up one more article in the Declaration for discussion?" or "This is a vivid description, but do you think a courtly lady would express herself like this?" There were no grades given — grading in the usual sense does not exist in this school. Handing back the essays, the teacher said: "I think that together you have provided such a good background to the French Revolution that we ought to copy the essays in the form of a program to be handed out before the play." The students thought this was a good idea, but one of them objected: "We've written them so sloppily." Another suggested immediately that they should all take their essays home and rewrite them so they would look nicer. The suggestion was adopted by acclamation. The teacher had achieved his goal. The students themselves had decided to present a report that they would be able to feel proud of and satisfied with. For the rest of the session the pupils discussed how they should make the program text: some wanted to use calligraphy (which they had learned in their drawing classes), others wanted to write the usual way, but use a special lay out, supplying their own drawn illustrations, etc. The intensive discussion, which gave tips as to how one might go about it, arrived at a decision whereby everyone would decide for themselves what form of presentation they wanted for their contribution. It will be a fairly hefty program, for there are thirty-two students in the class, and most of them will be contributing several pages each!

"Will these students be able to give an account of the causes of the revolution and the chain of events in, let's say, one year's time?" we ask the teacher afterwards. "Some of them will be able to," is the answer, "but for others the only aspects and events that will remain vivid in their minds will be those that have touched them strongly in a personal way for various reasons. The work with the play and the accompanying program sheets naturally means that the revolution will have a very special meaning for all of them. What matters is not to know the historical course of events in great detail but to understand the context and the general consequences of the revolution. There are reference books if you need to know the details, and the students have learned how to use such aids."

The Role Of The Teacher

In the seventh grade the students have a teacher who has followed the same students from the first grade and who teaches all subjects, though music and shop courses are taught in cooperation with other teachers when necessary. When a group of students seems to need it in order for them to feel secure, their teacher follows them up into the eighth grade, but normally all teaching from grade eight onward is done by specialized teachers.

The pupils are supposed to have the same teacher for a long

time, and as far as possible the class is to consist of the same pupils during the first 10 years of school (the compulsory school lasts ten years and is followed by a voluntary two-year high school). Continuity in these respects is of fundamental importance to the students according to Waldorf pedagogy. The teacher should be like a parent, and during the first few school years should exert strong authority. This is thought to provide the pupils with security and to give them a platform from which they can eventually take responsibility for themselves and practice co-determination. Student democracy corresponding to that found in the Swedish public schools does not emerge until the seventh grade, after which point it becomes more and more pronounced. These ideas are based on Steiner's psychology of development, which generally shows substantial similarities with Piaget's theory of cognitive development.

The conveying of information via the teacher is in fact an expression of his/her authority, but these presentations are justified also on other grounds: nothing is so emotionally involving as an artful oral presentation. A speaker can tailor form and content to the experiences and dispositions of his/her listeners and be guided by signals from them. Printed media and above all broadcast media lack this flexibility, and this is why the latter are not used in this school. Not even an overhead projector is considered suitable as an aid. It is better to draw on the blackboard, allowing the picture to emerge apace with the oral presentation.

Teacher training in Waldorf pedagogics provides intensive training in rhetoric, and all teachers prepare their daily "presentation" conscientiously, so that each individual pupil will be captivated by it. Teachers are aided in this planning by Steiner's psychology of personality, a typology used to describe the members of the class. Each personality type is assumed to be captivated by certain formal tricks and certain themes, and features that appeal to individual pupils or small groups of pupils must therefore be "woven into" the presentation. But obviously the teacher must also tie the subject to relevant experiences, whether they be those of individual students or of the whole group. Every student must feel personally touched by one or more features of a presentation session, and in this way the teaching is individualized. The students then have to elaborate what the teacher has presented, both in groups and individually.

Elaborating and Reporting

The production of period booklets is one of the most important means for elaborating a subject of instruction. In the lower grades it is the only means, apart from group discussions. The period booklet is often so well structured in terms of content and so instructively illustrated that it can be used as material for reviewing. Students usually put a great deal of work into both the text and the illustrations, striving to put their personal stamp on it. In the upper grades they usually prepare a rough draft in school for the teacher to comment on and then produce a final version at home. These period booklets are saved; they constitute, it can be said, an important part of the students' schoolbooks. Other schoolbooks are texts of the sort that are usually considered books for outside reading. These are used primarily in Swedish and foreign-language classes.

The purpose of the report book is not, of course, merely to provide a correct summary of the content of the period. The work is intended to train the pupils to write such summaries and to learn the value of being able to summarize what they have learned and to put their thoughts in order. But the report form also gives opportunities to express their own ideas, to choose their form of expression, to create something of their own, and to experience the pride of having done so. The teacher therefore avoids evaluative comments that grade the students against each other. The above examples of comments on essays are typical. Teachers also avoid putting any pressure on their students to finish assignments on time. It is not so important to treat a theme within the planned time frames. It has not been fully treated until the students have had the time necessary to produce report booklets that are to their own satisfaction.

In "our" class they experimented with other forms for reporting on the French Revolution theme. Essay writing on certain topics is often included in the work on a period booklet, but primarily to give the student an opportunity to give expression to his/her own thoughts, not as a test of knowledge. Tests of the multiple-choice variety are totally at odds with the epistemological views of Waldorf pedagogy and are therefore taboo.

In the upper grades a broad spectrum of report forms are brought to bear, not least exhibitions. On the school's mezzanine new student exhibitions are constantly on display. During our visit there were a number of large consoles depicting the basic features of various political ideologies, illustrated by pictures of and statements by advocates of each, as interviewed by students in the twelfth grade. But a longer period can also result in a more comprehensive practical presentation which gives form to the theoretical principles that have been dealt with. One example is the theme of "alternative sources of energy," which led the students in wood and metal shop to construct huge models of power plants that utilize wind and wave energy. The models were then put on display for a few weeks, together with descriptions of how they work, their calculated efficiency, etc.

As we can see, different subjects are integrated to a high degree, and this integration makes it possible for students with different dispositions and abilities to contribute on equal terms. For example, the more theoretically gifted can choose tasks that suit them while others can deal with more practical ones.

The displaying of period booklets, the exhibitions, plays, etc. also fill the function of serving as examples for the younger pupils. For this reason, too, it is important that students produce them with care. The older students are aware of this. Each and every one of the upper classes is a "buddy" to one of the lower classes, and each student in these classes adopts a younger pupil. Buddies look after their protégés at recess, and now and then they serve as teacher's aids in some of the buddy group's classes. Among other things, they usually teach their protégés how to knit. Both boys and girls know how, and you often see them doing their knitting during recess and off-hours!

Characterizing Evaluations Instead of Grading

In all Waldorf schools marking is done in the form of individually characterizing judgments about each student. These evaluations take into consideration the student's own abilities and describe not only the student's achievement but also his/her disposition and conduct. The report card is called a "school year letter" and in the lower grades it is addressed to the parents. Starting from the sixth year of school it is usually directed to the students themselves. The school-leaving certificate is formulated to include what prospective employers would want to know. In Sweden university admissions are based on marks according to the graduated scale prescribed for public schools. Therefore Waldorf schools issue such grades as well if the student plans to apply for university studies.

A school-year letter contains first of all a general comment on the pupil's conduct, for example, this one from the sixth grade:

> I'm delighted to see that B has started to raise his hand often and to express himself eagerly. When his oral contribution is needed in the group, however, he demonstrates great passiveness. He still has a hard time standing up straight. What I would like to see in grade 7 is for you to resolve to do your best with the things you find difficult.

Then follows a description of how the pupil has related to each school subject, for example:

> *Swedish*: B has made great progress during the year in spelling and composition writing. He has fought an uphill battle with his penmanship, but he is now developing a better hand. B has done well in grammar.

> *Botany*: B has a vivid interest in plants and has made many fine drawings of flowers in his workbook. His knowledge is good.

Waldorf pedagogy rejects all kinds of competition among pupils. Competition is at odds with cooperation, and it counteracts social belonging. Graduated marking is therefore outlawed, as are all sorts of competitive features of lessons (also in physical education and sports). Nevertheless, the teachers face an uneven battle with the pupils' — not least the youngest boys' — interest in competitive team sports, like soccer and ice hockey.

Varying Group Sizes

During the period classes in the mornings, the whole class is always assembled. Provided the teacher has mastered the art of presenting material, the size of the group does not matter, and when the students produce their period booklets it is in fact an advantage, say the Waldorf theoreticians, to have a group that is large and made up of students with varying dispositions and aptitudes. Variation and pluralism in a group is thought to enhance productivity. Of course, the teacher must have the time to help individual students, but from the first year in school much emphasis is placed on teaching pupils to help each other and to seek help and inspiration from their classmates. The classroom environment should be permeated by a feeling of cooperation, and in this respect, too, the more advanced pupils should serve as models for the others.

In proficiency lessons, however, the class is often divided in two. This is not least the case when it comes to language instruction, where training in oral communication requires smaller and more homogeneous groups to be effective, but it can also be necessary for proficiency training in mathematics, for example, where the teacher has to provide lots of individual help. But expressions like giftedness differentiation are not used; the rationale behind group divisions primarily revolves around practical considerations.

The Importance of Handicrafts and Art

One of the most visible features of Waldorf schools is the prominent role assigned to the arts.

First and foremost there are many subjects in the timetable that are related to artistic endeavor: painting, drawing, music, choir, orchestra, drama, art history, eurhythmics (a special kind of creative dance). Artistic subjects also include ceramics, textile shop, and wood and metal shop. Not all grade levels have all of these subjects in their schedules, but on the other hand artistic activities are integrated with most other subjects.

In the lower grades they play the flute every day for a while in the morning period. Singing and poetry recitation are included in many subjects throughout school, but especially during the first few years. Once a month the morning is devoted to a student production for everybody in the assembly hall (the monthly festival). The school orchestra gives a concert, certain classes perform choral music, dances, or short skits, and individual pupils play instruments, sing, and recite.

In knowledge-based subjects, in which students produce period booklets, drawing and painting is included as a natural part, and it is seen as a way to keep lessons from becoming too intellectually top-heavy. The ideal is a balance between concentrated thinking and creative expression. Handicrafts and artistic efforts offer students an opportunity to give physical expression to their feelings. Children have a deeply rooted need for such expression, since the corporeal and the spiritual are intimately joined in them. At Kristoffer School crafts and artistic pursuits are therefore *also* used as therapy for pupils who are tired of school or depressed. They have the possibility of replacing the school subjects that they have no enthusiasm for with augmented teaching in handicrafts for about a month in an attempt to "find themselves." But this is not a form of punishment: on the contrary, the pupils themselves must apply for augmented handicrafts, and their arguments are carefully scrutinized by the staff. This is the only form of special instruction that exists at Kristoffer School.

One of the first things a visitor notices and asks about at a Waldorf school is why students' paintings are based on prismatic colours and seem to have a certain common style. In order to "liberate" those children who are inhibited, timid, or afraid of making mistakes, the first-grade pupils are taught a number of technical tricks. One of the aids is painting with water colours on wet paper. No pre-drawn sketches can be used since the paint spreads out, blurring contours and mixing colours where they meet. The pupils are creating something, but not something based on a sketch. In other words, they can never fail! The choice of colours is the other aid. Five colours are quite sufficient for a beginner. They use pure yellow, warm vermilion, cooler crimson, ultramarine, and Prussian blue. Since the colours blend together in the border areas on the moistened paper, the students eventually learn spontaneously how to produce green, brown, violet, gray, etc. with these five colours.

Children are "born expressionists" and like to turn things they have heard or seen into pictures, but they do not strive for faithful realism. Therefore, they should be encouraged to paint directly, without contours. Since all pupils learn to use these five colours in this way, they develop a common style.

A Coherent Pedagogical Theory

The period teaching, the forms for reporting, the "buddy" system, the artistic activities, etc. are *examples* of methodological features of Waldorf pedagogy. It also comprises a number of other idiosyncrasies, all of which derive from the same theory; indeed, even the architecture and color scheme of Kristoffer School have their roots in this theory. However, it would take far too much space to give an account of even the fundamentals of the theory, that is, the anthroposophic system of thought. It is more relevant in this connection to consider how Waldorf pedagogics can maintain its uniqueness and still develop. A key to this is how the staff works.

Staff Work

It is the school's staff, consisting of all of the teachers it employs, that bears the responsibility for its pedagogical activities. Most of the staff members are members of the school's foundation, which has the economic responsibility. (The roughly thirty Waldorf schools that exist in Sweden are private, but the state and local governments contribute eighty-five percent of the cost the schools' pupils would have incurred in the public school system. At the same time, the schools often have their own funds and charge a tuition fee, albeit a low one.)

The staff meets every week for five hours during an afternoon and evening. Moreover, they have planning days after the end of the school year and preparations before each new school year to determine schedules and common activities.

The staff conference comprehends pedagogical studies, the presentation of a class and/or experiences from teaching a certain subject or theme, student issues of a general sort, topical matters regarding monthly festivals, plays, outdoor activities, field trips, etc.

The staff can be said to be the heart of the pedagogical work. The staff and each of its members bear full responsibility for decisions taken. The school has no principal whose word might carry more weight than that of other teachers. The staff members enjoy full equality, although different teachers obviously bring with them special experience from their own subject area. There is no gradation of the degree of responsibility, apart from occasions when one or more staff members have been appointed to carry out a special assignment. The school's salary system contributes to the cooperative atmosphere. The salary is the same for all teachers, though bonuses are given according to need, depending for example, on the size of family the teacher supports.

The agenda usually includes some theme from Steiner's writings, which is brought down to earth in the form of pedagogical questions. After this discussion, a teacher might tell about a work period in a certain subject and illustrate the talk with the students' period booklets or describe the situation of a pupil who has been having problems in school. There is no rush, and everyone tries to empathize, dwelling on details and offering opinions. The purpose of the discussion is to further the theoretical and methodological schooling of everyone so that theory and action can be melded into one and so there is no deviation from the theoretical underpinnings. In other words, what individuals have seen and heard is juxtaposed with the overriding theory, so that the action can either be justified by it or so that the action will follow another avenue in the future. This scrutiny of the behaviour of each individual and his/her rationale for it entails the schooling of each one in the theory and its consequences, but it also leads to each and every one participating in the work of the others, becoming familiar with the school's classes and individual pupils, learning how different teachers go about their work, getting useful ideas for their own work, etc. Visitors are struck not only by how similarly all of the school's teachers argue about various educational questions but also by how familiar each teacher is with how people teach different subjects and with all the students in the school, despite their relatively high number.

The rest of the time the staff splits into smaller groups, for example, by grade level, to treat more specific matters that might demand immediate attention.

Students and parents have little influence on the pedagogical activities. To be sure, the staff willingly listens to proposals for change, but only those which are compatible with Waldorf theories will be accepted, otherwise the theories might be sullied within a short space of time. If the parents do not accept the school's policy, then their only recourse is to remove their child from the school. There are, in fact, some "perennial" items of contention. One example has to do with when a pupil should learn to read. In Waldorf schools reading starts late — not until the end of the second or beginning of the third year —when the child is nine years old. There are theoretical reasons for this, and in fact during the first couple of years the instruction is to a great extent geared to preparing the child for reading, but parents refer to the fact that children in the public schools start learning to read in the first grade, and they are concerned that their children will "get behind." There are also cases where parents have succeeded in changing the work of the school, but in those cases the staff's careful consideration has proven the suggestions to be in harmony with the theories.

Thus, innovative ideas come both from individual staff members and from outsiders, but they are always subjected to rigorous review.

In other questions that fall outside the realm of educational theory, however, both students and parents exert a great influence. There are a dozen different bodies in which they are represented and which deal with specific questions, such as, resolving conflicts between parents and the school, arranging parental education — so that parents will understand the school's objectives and methods before they enroll their children there, running campaigns against smoking and narcotics, etc.

Questions For Critical Reflection

1. **The school philosophy.** The most striking difference vis-à-vis traditional schools is the fact that there is a school philosophy, embraced by all the school's teachers and permeating all its operations, from its forms of organization and leadership to the individual teachers' approach to their colleagues and pupils. The teachers are schooled in anthroposophical ideas, sometimes from childhood and in other cases via teacher

training. The function of the staff work is thus to maintain and implement this philosophy in practical action as well as to deepen and expand the individual's knowledge of it.

If so much energy must be expended on this, is it then reasonable to think that a normal group of teachers will be able to both develop and sustain a specific, uniform school philosophy?

2. **What do the students learn?** Most Kristoffer School parents are not anthroposophists, and their children do not become anthroposophists either. They seldom abandon the religious creed of their home —be it Orthodox Judaism, Protestant or Catholic Christianity, or Mohammedanism — despite the fact that anthroposophy is anti-religious. On the other hand, pupils cannot avoid being influenced by the values that pervade their education or adopting the attitudes the school attempts to inculcate in them. For example, they tend to be against competition, market-economic thinking, "consumer society," etc., often maintaining emphatically that the principle of equal pay should be applied universally. If they become farmers, they tend to take up biodynamic cultivation, and the scientifically oriented tend to have a penchant for working with the exploitation of alternative sources of energy. School imparts not only knowledge; students incorporate values and develop attitudes. Often both teachers and students are unaware of this.

Students at Waldorf schools adopt values that are in many ways incompatible with those that currently dominate Western societies. Their school offers them a conception of society and a view of humankind and knowledge that differs from what traditional schools stand for. Is this desirable, considering the students' future roles as citizens in society? How revolutionary can a school be?

3. **Should one teacher stay with a class for seven years?** Waldorf teachers teach a class all subjects for the first seven years of school. What advantages and disadvantages may result from this policy compared to receiving a new teacher every year?

4. **Should the introduction of reading be deferred until age nine?** Waldorf teachers present all themes orally, with their own drawings to illustrate, until students are nine years old. Then reading is introduced and used. What are advantages and disadvantages of this policy?

Related Readings

Allen, P. M. (1970). *Education as an art.* Blanvert, N.Y.: Rudolf Steiner Publication.

Carlgren, F. (1976). *Education towards freedom: Rudolf Steiner education.* East Grinstead, U.K.: Lanthorn Press.

Childs, G. (1991). *Steiner education in theory and practice.* Edinburgh, U.K.: Floris Books.

Harwood, A. C. (1979). *The way of a child.* London: R. Steiner Press.

Richards, M. C. (1980). *Toward wholeness: Rudolf Steiner education in America.* Middletown, Conn.: Weslyan University Press.

Chapter Seven

A Self-Evaluating Classroom

Merle Kennedy in collaboration with Joanne Randall

Introduction

I was introduced to Joanne's work in 1991. At that time I was studying with Chuck Chamberlin at the University of Alberta and he was familiar with Joanne's work in the classroom. I first wrote about her classroom in collaboration with three other writers as part of an article entitled *Dealing With Teacher Pain* (Henderson et al., 1991). This chapter expands upon that writing to describe in detail Joanne's evaluative practices and the philosophical underpinnings of those practices.

Our conversations took place over several months. Lapses in this dialogue were occasioned by our busy lives at home and at work. These conversations travelled backward and forward in time and sometimes they were anchored in the present. The writing that has resulted represents Joanne's work in the classroom over a fifteen year period and in two of her publications (Randall, 1990, 1991). During that time Joanne has taught at the elementary level from year one to year six and materials, strategies and processes from those experiences are used to illustrate her practice in this chapter.

Establishing A Context For Joanne's Work

Joanne's evaluative practices are very much a reflection of who she is and the sense of journey that she brings to her work:

> On reflection I see how I have travelled and continue to wander along both linear and recursive routes, moving forward but always going back to reflect, revise and re-evaluate upon what I have done and where I have been. (Randall, 1990, p.30)

Her personal metaphor of journey is one that she applies to her own development as a teacher. There is a sense of wholeness about her work because her sense of evaluation incorporates her work as a teacher as well as the work of her students. She establishes performance goals for herself within a given school year based on her students' needs and on her own professional development needs.

Working with year two students, Joanne wrote as a performance goal based on students' needs, "to provide a differentiated math program to meet the varying abilities of the class. To raise the class mean to a higher level of competency." She assessed her work in this area as follows:

1. I pretested the students on each unit then diagnosed it [the test]. By doing so I was able to identify which students master a concept(s) and which required more help and/or instruction ... sometimes I taught only 2–3 kids, 6–8 kids, or 20 kids. For those kids who had shown mastery I provided:

   - an enrichment math centre,
   - a manipulative/games centre at which they worked independently (when shown how to)...

2. For those children having extreme difficulty (2 in my case) I tutored their parents on how to use certain strategies and manipulatives at home to reinforce the concepts being taught at school.... For all students, I communicated, both verbally and in class newsletters to parents the importance of spending 5 min. each day drilling their children on addition and subtraction basic facts.

3. I also used peer teaching to reinforce teacher instruction.... My class mean [55/60] was above [the] system mean [53.3/60].... my main concern when determining this objective was for several weak students. I feel I provided as best I could a differentiated program to meet all their varying needs.

This approach to goal setting, completing tasks to achieve the goals, and evaluating progress has also been the central element in Joanne's teaching philosophy, and has been explicitly applied to facilitating children's growth toward becoming self-directed inquirers and learners.

Teachers must take a greater responsibility for the establishment of climate and philosophy. Joanne's work is centered in her classroom. She has discovered that students who are happy and successful tell their parents they are happy and successful and the children become the advocates of her program and philosophy. Her classroom operates on an open-door policy; the principal and parents are welcome. The classroom is alive with students' work and students talking about their learning. At the beginning of the year she has an open house to explain the program and asks for parent input. This input consists of positive aspects of the learning environment and constructive criticism. At this time of the year parents are also asked to complete a questionnaire to assist Joanne in better planning a program for their child. Two important questions that are a part of this questionnaire follow:

1. What kinds of development do you think are important for your child?

2. What suggestions can you give for meeting your child's needs in school?

There is also the importance she places on expanding her work, "I see myself moving through not only my classroom as a centre for learning but throughout the school and even beyond. My classroom is open to any teacher. I have encouraged interclass visitations from colleagues who are excited by the happenings in my class ..." (Randall, 1990, p. 33). Within the school, Joanne and her students share their work through student assemblies and interclass interactions. Her understanding of the school context also includes parental involvement and support.

She is guided by her personal teaching philosophy, a philosophy she first experienced as a guiding intuitive sense about children and which she now expresses as:

> ... empower[ing] my students to their fullest, individual potential.... I had been trying to provide a program which allowed and promoted independence, interaction and integration. I had been trying to use teaching methods and strategies by which the students could assume the learning responsibilities that were rightfully theirs. (Randall, 1990, p. 31)

As an example of empowerment the excerpt below is taken from a progress report and is taped on the student's desk as a daily visual reminder.

The intent is to involve child, parents and teacher in conferences to set goals for future learning. Both the child and parents are encouraged to take responsibility for emphases in future learning activities.

Classroom Description

Each new year in Joanne's classroom begins with the development of a classroom creed. The purpose of the classroom creed is to create an effective learning environment where students take responsibility and ownership for their learning and their behaviour. As an example, the classroom creed developed and signed by her students during one year read as follows:

We Believe ...

- we should challenge our minds and bodies
- we should take pride in our work
- we should be able to work well independently or in a group
- we should take responsibility for everything we say and do
- we should have a warm, caring and supportive environment

- we should respect our teachers and fellow students
- we should be the best we can be
- we should respect our own and others' property and feelings
- we should have a neat, efficient, clean and cheery classroom
- we should treat others the way we would like to be treated

The desks are organized in clusters of four. A desk or two distinctly separate from these groups are chosen by those students who prefer to work independently. The identity of the desk's occupant is contained in a removable drawer. Every six to eight weeks, these clusters change occupants as the students once again decide how they want to spend this next period of time, individually or collectively. Taped in the upper right-hand corner of each desk is a list of goals. Student, teacher and parents have set out these goals and discussed them. Joanne's experience is that goals should be concrete and specific. It is these kinds of goals that facilitate measurement so that growth and learning are more evident to all involved. The goals set by the student are different from those of the teacher and parents. There has been no need for consensus. There are exceptions, however. Special needs children need more structure and guidance and so Joanne is more involved in assisting these children in setting their own student goal(s).

Specific Teaching Activities And Methods

Assessment, the critiquing of work within curricular guidelines, must involve students. They are involved in two different ways, self-reflection and assessment and also peer reflection and peer assessment. This type of assessment lends itself to major projects and activities.

One wall of this classroom houses bookshelves filled with various books and binders. There is a binder for each student and it contains a wealth of evaluative material placed there by both the teacher and the student. The profile binder documents a student's work and serves as a basis for evaluation. In it are the student's achievements and reflections upon the achievement of his or her goals. This is contained at the beginning of the binder because of its focus on student self-esteem and self-assessment.

The remainder of the binder contains information about the student's progress in Math, Writing, Spelling, Science, and Social Studies. The profile binder also includes an interest inventory, contracts, and formal test results. There are photographs of projects completed or in process, and of the student engaged in a variety of activities, in-class as well as extra-curricular. Each teacher would index his/her binders according to his/her classroom program.

This binder is the key to student-parent-teacher conferences at which time each student proudly displays and discusses the process and product of his or her classroom inquiries. The parents write down goals they would like to see themselves or have their children work on. The following are examples of parental goal-setting:

Parent Goal: 15 min. oral reading 2X week, 15 min. spelling 2X week, 3X week — letter writing; rereading, editing — 30 min or self-directed selected writing.

Parent Goal: Help Soreiya master basic facts and develop study skills.

Parent Goal: We would like Alison to continue to improve her math skills and keep up the excellent work in her Reflections book.

Parent Goal: I will try to work at daily assignments with Kent.

Parent Goal: To assist Tanis in mastering her basic facts, and encourage her to complete her homework and assignments.

Each child sets goals, in addition to the teacher who sets goals based on the child's strengths and weaknesses and personal interests. Each feels shared responsibility in the collaborative process of goal setting.

In one corner of the room is a round table where three boys are engaged in a simulation of an archeological dig. Each is gently hammering at plaster-of-paris chunks with embedded broken plates and artifacts. These boys are enjoying the hammering as they chat about how the parts fit together. Physical, social and intellectual activity are all going on simultaneously. Joanne is videotaping this activity as part of the ongoing recording of learning activities and as a means of sharing what is happening in the classroom with the parents. The other students read quietly so as not to interfere with the recording.

When the taping ceases, the rest of the students begin work on their chosen goals. Setting goals helps them answer the question, "What would you like to learn about?" They use this time for two purposes. First, they will find out about their chosen topic by using a wide variety of sources throughout the city. Second, they will work out the best method of presenting what they have learned to students in their class and, in some cases, other students in their school.

Students have investigated such topics as recycling, fashion design, synchronized swimming, rocks and minerals and photography. Their sources of information vary and include relevant agencies, such as provincial associations, local businesses and first-hand accounts. Their presentations include field trips, guest speakers, learning centres and games. The following example is taken from Joanne's work with a year two class:

> As part of the unit [on peace] the students wrote letters expressing their concerns with world peace and disarmament to Prime Minister Brian Mulroney, Premier Don Getty, Mayor Laurence Decore or [Doug] Roche. And although most responded in written form, Roche found the time to drop by and discuss the issue with students. (Logie, 1988)

Sometimes the outcome of a student's inquiry is the formation of a club where those whose interest has been sparked by another student's inquiry can meet and jointly pursue their newfound interest.

Joanne's evaluative practices "more effectively communicate both program planning and the monitoring and demonstrating of student growth" (Randall, 1991). The following components of her evaluative process also speak to her personal philosophy of empowering students.

1. **Program Planning** — to establish goals for each student based on his or her strengths and weaknesses.

2. **Student Goals** — to motivate and enrich learning based on the student's interests, as well as give ownership of learning to the student.

3. **Home Goals** — to reinforce the partnership between home and school by working together to provide the best educational program for the student.

4. **Parent Goals** — to provide input into their child's program.

5. **Reflections** — to think about what has been learned, how it was learned, and how it can be applied to a new situation. Reflections give information which both the student and the teacher can use to monitor and direct his/her course of learning. This process further equips the teacher to be a mentor, facilitatior and co-discoverer in the student's development.

6. **Video Evaluations/Video Newsletters** — Video evaluations are a new assessment tool to reflect the active nature of learning. Video newletters are a more current technological medium for transmitting the goings-on of the classroom to parents and the community.

7. **Profile Binder** — a collection of representative work by the student. The profile binder is a kind of resume which serves to document students' work and growth and which serves as a basis for evaluation.

Critique Of Traditional Schooling

What underlies all of this is the students' assumption of responsibility for planning and carrying out the inquiry and its follow-up. The room is filled with a productive hum as students help one another with these projects. Joanne acts as a facilitator, moving among the clusters of students to answer questions and share ideas. Some students are preparing outlines that will be due very shortly. Others are searching through magazines for pictures, and some students are trying out parts of their presentations on fellow students.

The rationale that underpins this structure is clearly communicated to parents. They, too, support the educational aim of empowering students by providing an atmoshpere that allows for individual growth and the assumption of individual responsibility to plan for that growth. There is student and parent involvement in the entire process from planning through to evaluation. The following are some parents' comments on conferences, motivation, parental influence, and general reaction.

Parent A: The transition for "Parent/Teacher Interview" to "Student/Parent/Teacher Conference" was a refreshing change. I believe it is highly valuable to allow and encourage the child's input. Reviewing and talking about their own strengths helps promote enthusiasm, and builds self esteem. Vocalizing their weaknesses and areas for improvement really forces them to use their own minds. This could be a first step toward self improvement for anyone.

The quality of motivation has been higher. Threats, or fear of failure can be strong motivaters but the long term results are not always positive.

Setting goals is an important part of everyone's life.

The school appears to have an "Open-Door" policy, and parental input is welcomed.

We were advised the Strathcona Science Park would enhance our son's project on Archaeology. We plan to visit there as soon as weather permits. We were grateful for the suggestion.

Moving our son from one school to another midway through the year was a difficult decision. Our only regret now, is that he could not have been in your program sooner.

Your program has been an Education on Education. Thank you.

Parent B: I feel that children who are able to be proud of their accomplishments will excel and succeed because they have been allowed to feel good about accomplishments and goals. It also allows the child to feel comfortable and not uneasy with teacher and parents sitting there. Sometimes we as parents place so much value on test results that we do not recognize areas that our child might excel in.

With our child the emphasis was on marks in her previous school. Unfortunately she did not do as well as peers; she was down on herself and felt she could not succeed. Since entering Mrs. Randall's class we have seen a more confident young lady emerge.

We were always aware of what was going on in our daughter's class as she took an active interest in everything Mrs. Randall did. We did not however do any of the above (teacher suggestions).

You have done a wonderful job in fostering Lisa's ability to realize that she can be or can do anything she sets her mind to.

Parent C: This is an excellent way to start the conference since it shows what Tanya has learnt and how she feels about it. It also teaches the child to talk about what she is learning and brag about her work. It is the child's education and she should be involved and have a say in what she is learning and how.

Goal setting has helped Tanya aim at what she knew she could strive for. She always kept her goals for certain projects pinned up in her room. Goal setting has not only motivated Tanya but also changed the way she thinks when trying to accomplish tasks.

Tanya's excitement towards her year in the Grade 5 program has brought learning and has motivated our involvement in her education. We have gone on many library trips and weekend outings which were directly related to a school project which was in the program.

This method of teaching and involvement has improved Tanya's love for learning and has given her some *strong* skills which I know she will carry forward through her education. Reflecting on what was being learnt and why has developed Tanya's learning process. I know this was one of her best years in school as far as enjoyment and development.

In this classroom, the student is of primary importance. Rather than forcing students to be slaves to the curriculum, the curriculum becomes the students' servant. Acknowledging this frees Joanne from the technical control of the curriculum.

Prescribed texts are considered as one of many resources, not the one and only resource these students use. Since the students take responsibility for their learning, these resources must be varied to best meet their interests and learning styles. Students learn to reach out into the broad community to get needed information from people who have expertise, just as adults do.

Joanne's concept of evaluation has expanded to include a variety of evaluative techniques. The students share the responsibility for their own evaluation, as well as evaluation of classmates' work. Such sharing empowers the students because they are allowed to take responsibility for their efforts. One device is an evaluation form for students to complete after working through the activities at another student's centre. A second form is for students' self-evaluation of their own independent projects.

Student Centre Evaluation

Name of Centre:

Evaluated By:

1. What I liked about your centre...

2. From working through your centre I learned...

3. Problems I had with the centre...

4. Suggestions...

Indpendent Projects – Reflections

1. What steps did you go through to complete your project?

2. What strategies did you use?

3. What strategies did you learn?

4. What difficulties did you experience? How did you overcome them?

5. What went well for you? Why?

6. What feelings did you experience over the course of this project? Give specific examples and why you felt the way you did.

7. What do you know now that you never knew before completing your project?

8. What would you do differently if you were to do the project over again?

9. What will the other students learn from your project? Will they enjoy your project? Why or why not? List your reasons.

10. Networking: Draw a flow chart indicating who you networked with and what service or information they provided you.

Joanne's classroom is not rule-bound. The rules arise to meet particular situations in the classroom and are subject to discussion and change. The atmosphere in the classroom is one of cooperation, confidence and ease among the students and between the students and the teacher.

Joanne's openness to genuine dialogue and to a sharing of directions frees her from the pain that often results from teacher-centered teaching. A community of trusting and caring results, which helps ensure relevance and involvement for her and her students. The responsibilty for schooling is shared. Since the students are involved in the selection of their own goals, her role is to help the students by working with them to attain these goals. The students have learned to replace, "Why bother?" with "How might it be? Let's make it so." She has created an atmosphere in which the student, in cooperation with the teacher, determines what is relevant knowledge, how to get it and what it is used for.

Conclusion

Joanne has shared her journey with the hope that other teachers will:

- explore alternative ways of assessing student growth
- empower their students
- promote self-directed learning
- promote student success
- examine their beliefs about assessment
- align their beliefs and their practices
- build a strong partnership among students, parents, and teachers

It is the examination of her own evaluative practises on student assessment that have led to some of the findings that she has shared. Her evaluative practises are a work in progress, they continue to evolve. She does not have all the answers but she does hope that teachers begin the process of critiquing their current practises on student assessment.

Questions For Critical Reflection

1. How can you demonstrate student growth without using paper and pencil techniques?

2. How do you empower your students?

3. In what processes can you involve your students to facilitate self-reflection? self-evaluation? peer evaluation?

4. How can you promote and encourage the home and school partnership?

References

Access Network (1992). *Evaluation* [Video]. Edmonton: Access.

Access Network (1992). *Program continuity: Principles into practice — making connections in the upper grades.* [Video and Manual]. Edmonton: Access.

Henderson, B., Kennedy, M., Sabo, L. & Chamberlin, C. (1991). "Dealing with teacher pain," *The ATA Magazine, 71* (3), 9–13.

Logie, G. (1988, January 10). "Roche replies ro [sic] children's concerns with visit," *Edmonton Examiner*.

Randall, J. & Hayden, R. (1990). "Back to the future: One teacher's journey to literacy empowerment," *Early Childhood Education, 23*, 30–33.

Randall, J. (1991). Profiling student growth: A teacher manual. Edmonton: Trinity Press.

Chapter Eight

Montessori Teaching In Swedish Compulsory Schools

Christina Gustaffson

Introduction

This article deals with Montessori teaching in Swedish schools.
Maria Montessori (1870–1952) was born in Italy. She was the
first woman in Italy to become a medical doctor. Her first job
was at a psychiatric clinic and after that she became the leader
of a school for mentally retarded children. Montessori found
that these hopelessly deficient children could learn a lot of
things and she asked herself why mentally normal children
couldn't perform more than they usually could. She got the
opportunity to answer her own question about normal children's performance when she became the leader of a full-time
pre-school in a slum district of Rome. In her pre-school, called
"Casa Dei Bambini" (Children's House), she combined her
great theoretical knowledge with practical work, which was
soon to be known all over the world.

In spite of the fact that Montessori had devoted herself to
work at hospitals, studying philosophy and psychology resulted in becoming a Professor in anthropology. She then chose to

develop her educational method through practical educational work. The greater part of her life she devoted to Montessori schools and Montessori societies and of course to train teachers in her method. Consequently she started a period of forty years of moving to many countries, both inside and outside of Europe, to participate in conferences and to give a lot of lectures and teacher training courses. But she also had time for scientific development work. This was spread in her books and articles. Her major books, however, were published before 1920. Later writings under her name are often transcribed lectures or translations of lecture notes. Montessori had her last home in Holland where she died in 1952.

Montessori is known as an educator and the founder of a teaching method. Her work was, however, deeper and wider than that of an educator. Every single part of her pedagogy is related in a certain way to the wholeness of the child, and her message, a result of a lifework, envelops the whole child. The most decisive finding was that the child, in a continual state of growth, was sensitive to different stimuli at various stages of learning. Montessori's very solid theoretical studies complemented her practical experiences to form a unique knowledge about the child's mental development and capacity to learn. The systematic knowledge about the learning process was a pre-requisite for the principles for teaching, i.e. the Montessori method.

The development of the Montessori method happened during the first decade of the 20th century. The basic principles, however, are general and independent of chronology. That is why the fundamental parts of the method are the same today as in the beginning of this century.

Most of her time Montessori worked with small children (3–7 years) and developed theories about their learning and guidelines for their teaching. The access to Montessori schools for small children has been better than for older children during the whole of the 20th century. But the Montessori method is used at primary and intermediate levels too. Montessori herself was of the opinion that her discoveries were applicable up to university age. However, when the children are more than 12 years old there is no real Montessori teaching, but one can find teaching inspired by Montessori's basic principles at lower and upper secondary levels.

In Sweden the interest in the Montessori method has changed over time. Already in the 1930s there were Montessori schools in Sweden. In the year 1987, however, the interest in Montessori rose. It was an anniversary year in the international history of Montessori education, because it was 80 years since Montessori started her first school. Another event was that one of the most important books written by Montessori was translated into Swedish. But in Sweden the most important event was that a Montessori teacher training course was started. Certainly, it was a course for 3–6 year old children. But a consequence of this was that parents and teachers now want Montessori schools for older children. Therefore there has been an increase of Montessori classes, grades 1–6, during the last few years.

Before this alternative teaching method is described, it is necessary for me to describe what Montessori teaching is an alternative for.

Knowledge About Teaching In Swedish Classrooms[1]

This section is a summary of some results from research on teaching conducted in Sweden during the last two decades. Firstly, Swedish classroom researchers have found rather one-sided teaching methods. The whole-class teaching has been predominate. In some studies three quarters of the time have been devoted to whole-class teaching. The teacher steers and the class follows him/her. Swedish classroom researchers have also found the quantitative pattern of the so called two-thirds rule. This means that the teacher's share of utterances in the classroom is two-thirds, while all the pupils are responsible for only one-third. This third part can further be divided in two thirds plus one third. About three or four pupils, often boys, are usually responsible for the two-thirds and the rest of class, perhaps 20–25 pupils are responsible for one-third. This pattern becomes more marked when we are counting words uttered in the classroom. The teacher-pupil ratio with regard to spoken words is 75% to 25%.

The "normal" interaction in a classroom has also been very

stereotyped. It is simple and brief. Most often the teacher puts the questions and the pupils answer these questions. Sometimes the teacher reacts to the questions. The communication becomes technical and unnatural.

In most Swedish classrooms the teaching aids, especially textbooks, are important for both teachers and pupils. They often don't follow the logic of the subject and are written in obscure language.

It is also evident that it is difficult for the teacher to individualize in terms of different qualitative treatment between pupils. An ambition to deal with different individual demands often results in a quantitative difference. That is, the teacher repeats almost the same sentence two, three or more times, when the pupil in fact needs another approach to the problem.

Of course the above description is strongly simplified and summarized. But the similarities between the Swedish experiences and the description given in the first chapter in this publication are striking. In Sweden many individual teachers and the staff of whole schools have noticed that there is some truth in this description, and they know that this is not consistent with the goals of the Swedish curriculum. A number of the teachers have investigated possible educational alternatives without going outside the curriculum goals. The Montessori method was one of these alternatives.

My own interest in Montessori teaching is more than twenty years old. Some years ago I got the opportunity to study Montessori teaching in two Swedish public schools. The description of the milieus and of the special Montessori teaching sequences below is taken from this study.

Some Impressions From Montessori Classrooms, Grades 1–6

The school is a public one and only a small part of it applies the Montessori method. Grades 1–6 are involved. But there are not six Montessori classes, because Montessori teaching is non-graded. The marking of the grade is less important. However, sometimes it is practical for the pupils to know that they belong to Grade 1, Grade 2, etc. Sometimes it is also practical for the teacher to gather pupils who are of the same age. In such cases the Grades 1–3 and 4–6 usually work together in a Montessori school. In this school they have another order. When the pupils are gathered in a "class," the Grades 1–2, 3–4 and 5–6 work together.

Standing outside the Montessori classroom the most noticeable thing you see is a row, or rather a heap, of shoes. When you come inside the classroom you observe that there are two more classrooms behind the first one. But the doors are open, so you can almost consider them as a very large room. A Montessori environment should invite meaningful activities. These rooms are unconventionally furnished if you compare with a normal classroom in Sweden. A rather large part of the floor is free from furniture. Some parts of the surface are covered by rugs. Of course there are tables, chairs, and cupboards, all constructed in proportion to dimensions and needs of the children and often placed along the walls. The furnishing allows collaboration between the pupils. Therefore there is no ambition to furnish in a way where the pupils are turned in the same direction, for instance toward the black board. Montessori also recognized that the environment should be attractive psychologically. This should include consideration about the room decorations such as flowers, colours, posters, curtains, etc., which you can find in this school.

The Montessori method is based upon three important principles — freedom, independent study, and individualization. Montessori herself emphasizes freedom as the most important principle of her method and says: "Let us leave the life *free* to develop within the limits of the good, and let us observe this inner life developing. This is the whole of our mission" (Montessori 1965, p. 134). "The fundamental principle of scientific pedagogy must be, indeed, the *liberty of the pupil*; — such liberty as shall permit a development of individual, spontaneous manifestations of the child's nature" (Montessori 1964, p. 28).

Thus, one basic principle of the method is that the child should be free to choose an exercise related to his mental development. In a Montessori classroom each child has his/her own curriculum. Physical exercises which can be more or less complex make way for an internal development: "In our efforts with the child, external acts are the means which stimulate internal development, and they again appear as its manifestation, the two elements being inextricably intertwined" (Montessori 1964, p. 353). The freedom to choose an activity and adequate material and the freedom to concentrate on the activity as long as it is necessary for learning demands a special organization of the environment.

One demand is a set of teaching material which allows the pupils to study at their own speed, to follow their own interests, and to choose their own study methods. To a certain extent there is also a demand that the material should be self-correcting. Many Montessori materials can be used by both younger and older pupils. For the older children Montessori constructed didactic material for exercises in language, reading, arithmetic, geometry, drawing, music, and metrics (Montessori 1973). The thought behind each piece of material was that each subject should be presented by means of external objects according to a well-defined systematic plan for learning. Step by step the child can pass in his/her own time from the concrete to the abstract in a sequence appropriate to his/her stage of development.

Thus in a Montessori classroom the didactic material, books, and the other teaching aids are essential. They should be placed where they are clearly visible and easy to reach even for the smaller children. It is also very important that the material is carefully arranged. Most often the children are expected to choose and identify the teaching aids without help from the teacher. In "my" Montessori school each subject has a special colour which means that the material for learning Swedish for instance, is situated in yellow boxes, yellow folders, etc.

Because of the size of the rooms and the pupils moving around you can't imagine that the number of pupils is about 50. They are also speaking in ordinary voices, but it is not troublesome. A few pupils are working on the rugs on the floor. They are, however, concentrating so completely that they don't notice that you are moving around them. There are three teachers in total. During almost the whole day in school the Montessori pupils are expected to do independent study individually or in a smaller group.

Sometimes one, two, or all three teachers gather a group of

pupils in the morning for a short talk about the work this day. Often the groups consist of pupils of different ages. When the groups disperse each pupil fetches the material they first are going to work with. Since it is characteristic for Montessori teaching that all material exist only in one copy, the pupils sometimes are forced to wait for their turn. Then they are expected to choose another material or task. For some of the pupils the school days start in another way. They walk very purposefully first to the shelves and the bookcases for fetching the material they are going to use. Before they sit down, each of them very shortly tells the teacher about the plans for the day.

Below I am going to present a few instantaneous pictures from "my" classrooms. They are my personal choice from a Montessori environment which I became familiar with. However, I have chosen these pictures because they are typical for a Montessori environment.

Today Mary (Grade 5) and John (Grade 6) look into a box filled with different technical things, a laborative preproduced teaching aid. The box also contains some cards. On each card there is an exercise which the pupils are expected to solve. Mary and John are looking at these cards rather randomly. After a short discussion they decide to solve the task titled "Lifting cranes and winches." This is a task which demands special previous knowledge. It is uncertain if these two pupils have this knowledge. (Some other tasks in this box are expected to be done before the chosen task. These cards have been sorted away by Mary and John.) However, this is no problem for these two pupils. They start building a working lifting crane. The strategy they are using is looking at the picture on the card, trying to identify the pieces, and trying to replicate. The task seems rather difficult. Neither Mary nor John are sure of any new decision. Now and then it is Mary who believes that she has identified something and eagerly throws herself over a component and tries it. Sometimes John does the same thing. The whole time they are discussing. But they seem to listen to each other with a low attention. From the beginning they have been very concentrated. Half an hour later without any form of break Mary and John have constructed a functioning lifting crane. Quickly they destroy it and choose another task.

Analyzing this episode from an educational perspective some things are worth noticing. Mary and John have been working for half an hour and no teacher has been involved, in spite of the fact that there have been three teachers around them. Certainly, my impression was that Mary and John didn't listen to each other the whole time, but there *was* a verbal interaction. And more important, it was a *natural* conversation between two pupils. Other remarkable things are that it was a collaboration between a boy and a girl of different ages and they initiated this task themselves, without knowing whether they could solve the task together. Their behaviour when the task was finished also indicated that they gave priority to process before product. All these things are rare in a normal classroom. It is also my opinion that the scenario as a whole is a positive one from the perspective of pedagogy, although maybe not every detail is positive? For instance, I couldn't evaluate their train of thought. The aim of the task — a concrete thing — can also be discussed.

Let me examine another episode:

An eight year old boy is sitting at a table. He is doing an exercise to learn the alphabet. After a while he becomes tired of this and starts cutting paper. He wants to construct a cube, but he discovers that he can't manage it. He asks the boy who is sitting beside him to come to his assistance. This boy is eleven years old. Immediately he lays down the book he is reading, takes the scissors and starts cutting and folding something which in a minute shows itself to be a cube. He also starts to fasten it with tape but asks the younger friend: "Don't you really want to tape?" He answers no, but he is very interested in his older friend's work. He is also anxious that there is not adhesive tape enough and he begins to look around find more. But there is tape enough and when he gets the completed cube he turns to me and tells me that he is going to paint it. He fetches water-colors, seems to ponder and asks his older friend: "Do you mind if I paint it with the black and yellow colors?" The answer is: "Not at all!"

My second episode is also an illustration of practical, experimental work. It is built on a real, but more important, a spontaneous collaboration between two children who happened to be close this day. It is worth noticing that there is a rather big difference of age. My own personal reaction in a Montessori classroom is that the adult has another status than in a normal classroom. I am not a teacher for small children, but when I visit a compulsory school and the teacher is busy, the children usually approach me to ask something or comment about something. In a Montessori classroom the classmates come to assistance before the adults, including the teacher(s). It is often a new experience for the Montessori teacher not to be believed to know best in the class. I have seen more examples of this:

> Thirteen pupils belonging to Grades 5 and 6 are in one of the three rooms. Most of them are sitting around tables and several are studying geography. Individually or together they have chosen a country or a part of a continent to study more deeply. In spite of the fact that both a teacher and I are very near, suddenly a pupil from Grade 5 turns to a pupil from Grade 6 and asks: "Can you tell me what the word radical means?" The answer comes immediately: "Well, it is a person who likes big changes."

Let us return to the episode before this last example. Does the younger boy learn something when the older boy is constructing a cube? Of course, it is difficult to establish. Perhaps he never is coming to use his knowledge about constructing a cube. But the situation has a social value. It was a form of collaboration, even if the older boy did the piece of work. Typical for a Montessori atmosphere is also that the pupils are not afraid to ask the nearest classmate for help.

Montessori teaching has often been criticized for being an individualistic form of teaching. Because of the pupils' permission to speed up their own studies, the Montessori method has been said to create an élite. The criticism has arisen in spite of the fact that one of the most important goals in a Montessori environment is the social training. The outcome of this continuous social training is that the pupils are expected to demonstrate being considerate, being helpful and absolutely not competing. My intention in choosing the above scenarios was to tell the reader something about the relationship between the pupils and also to show the attitudes the pupils have about assisting each other.

From the above examples a relevant question is what the

teachers are doing. Montessori herself was of the opinion that the teacher had a special role: "It is my belief that the thing which we should cultivate in our teachers is more the *spirit* than the mechanical skill of the scientist; that is, the *direction* of the *preparation* should be toward the spirit rather than toward the mechanism" (Montessori 1964, p. 9). Thus the Montessori teacher is more a supervisor and a catalyst of learning than a lecturer. "For this teacher we have substituted the *didactic material*, which contains within itself the control of errors and which makes auto-education possible to each child. The teacher has thus become a *director* of the spontaneous work of the children. She is not a *passive* force, a *silent* presence" (Montessori 1964, p. 370). From these quotations one can get the impression that a Montessori teacher never lectures. It is, however, a misunderstanding that there are no common activities in a Montessori classroom. One important task for the Montessori teacher is to gather a group of pupils and lecture. To train grammar Montessori constructed a lot of didactic material. In the example below the teacher is using components from a so called grammar box containing symbols for word classification.

> Nine pupils, all of them belonging to Grade 1, are sitting on the floor. Together with the teacher they are going to work with the group of nouns. The teacher exposes Montessori's symbols for indefinite article and noun. Each pupil constructs an example such as "a table," "a chair," etc. After that the teacher adds the symbol for adjective and the nine pupils construct a sentence with an adjective each. In the third exercise the teacher wants the pupils to think of a sentence which demands use of one symbol for indefinite article, two symbols for adjectives, and one symbol for noun. They are going to put up their hands when they have found such an example. One pupil shows a tendency to impatience because another pupil needs more time than the rest. Immediately the teacher starts a discussion about this behavior. She emphasizes that nobody is in a hurry and all of the pupils have time to wait for each other. This little exercise lasts for about a quarter of an hour. When the teacher is closing this exercise she also gives recommendations for different activities connected with learning grammar. But the frames for the pupils are very wide.

The above sort of common activities are always very well planned. But sometimes the situation demands a spontaneous gathering:

Eight pupils and four adults (myself included) are gathered on the floor because one of the teachers wants a talk about an event the day before. A supply teacher had been dissatisfied with the pupils. She had tried to have a class council and that didn't function. When the teacher tells the pupils this, they agree. They are also of the opinion that it went astray, but they can't explain why. The teacher tries to teach them that the class council is important for themselves. However, if the pupils are not interested in democracy, the teachers can come to the decisions. I found this discussion very calm and objective. The pupils got the knowledge of doing something wrong. But I am not sure they knew in what way. The way the pupils handled the discussion can also be seen as a mark of loyalty to the supply teacher in spite of her complaining about them.

The Montessori teacher is in the classroom to guide and plan the education for the child. Another essential part of the Montessori teacher role is that of the observer. The teacher is expected to use systematic observation of the pupils and then arrange the situation in a way which allows the child to learn as much as possible with a minimum of help except for the didactic material. Montessori called this optimal organization the *prepared environment* where a great part is the didactic learning material. The observation can be focused on the pupil's social behaviour, the way they are performing a special exercise, the way they are choosing the tasks, or the like. The notes the teacher takes are analyzed and compared to give a picture of each child and his/her needs. This information about the child's capacity to learn is the basis for the teacher when she is going to direct the child. In this sense you can say that the child is directing the teacher. Finally, the Montessori teacher has also, together with the pupils, the responsibility to keep all the materials in good condition.

Comments On Montessori Teaching As A Critique Of Traditional Teaching

What is the difference between Montessori teaching and "normal" Swedish teaching? According to the current Swedish curriculum for the compulsory school, some of the more important tasks are:

> that the pupils get the chance to obtain considerable knowledge and skills,
> that the pupils' desire to work is stimulated,
> that the pupils learn responsibility and consideration,
> that the pupils become accustomed to work in a good way, and
> that the pupils are brought up to act democratically.

Let us return to our introduction about Swedish teaching research results. In a "normal" classroom everybody very often is doing the same thing at the same time. Most of the time is also devoted to whole-class teaching. Then the teacher is the leader. One consequence of the fact that the leader is steering the activities, talking a lot while the pupils become passive, is students speak almost only when they are commanded. And most of the verbal exchange is between teacher and pupil. Within this restricted teaching process there are few divergent elements or activities. The pupils' chances to develop the ability to talk and write are also limited. These characteristics of the "normal" classroom are enough to realize that it can be difficult to reach the goals set out in the curriculum. The possibilities in a Montessori classroom are, however, different.

In a Montessori classroom the pupils take responsibility for their own studies. They have to develop self-discipline and self-motivation. They have to fill the day with purposeful activities, because there is nobody else who does it. The role of the teacher is "only" to guide the child to choose the activities they are ready for. When they are ready for the activities, they also enjoy the activities. During my research in Montessori classrooms, I classified the activities corresponding to about eight whole school days. I found that about 70% of the time was devoted to independent study. Almost all this time the pupils, individually or in small groups, were busy with different tasks. A little more than one quarter of the time was devoted to common teaching activities. But the teacher predominated less than half of this time. The teacher together with the pupils or a group of pupils had the responsibility for the rest of the common activities.

Thus, we can establish that the pattern of the teaching activities in a Montessori classroom differs from the "normal" classroom. Therefore the conditions for working according to the curriculum are considerably more favourable. The pupils enjoy school activities, probably because they always have time to finish a piece of work and because they choose tasks in relation to their previous knowledge. This also leads to good work routines. The teaching organization demands the pupils' responsibility for each other, for the environment, and for their own learning activities. There is also an ambition that democracy will be a natural part of the Montessori method.

Summary And Conclusions

One essential question you can put after reading about Montessori teaching, is why most of the Swedish schools use teaching methods which are neither consistent with the curriculum, nor promote the development of the children. My opinion is that there are three critical aspects in every teaching situation: goals and contents (teaching aids), time, and prerequisites of studies. These are steering the teaching process. Different ways to organize and look upon these "frame factors," result in different teaching/learning processes.

Of course, both "traditional" and Montessori teachers, sometimes together with the pupils, formulate short-term goals in the educational milieu respectively. But when the "traditional" teachers are planning before a new school year they often formulate goals for one year at a time. And they try to find textbooks and other material that are adequate for these goals. Associated with the formulating of goals is the timetable. Now all Swedish schools have the so called frame timetable. This means that the schools themselves decide about the distribution between different subjects and over years. These decisions affect, however, groups of pupils, often whole classes. The frame timetable for the Montessori pupil is individual. It is the pupil's time and the task is superior to the time. In a Montessori class the goals usually are formulated for longer periods than a semester or a school year, most often for three years but sometimes for six years. One consequence of this is another view of teaching materials. The Montessori teachers don't look for pre-produced textbooks for the whole class for instance. The textbook can never be the course. Another demand is that the teaching material shall reflect the logical building of each subject. That is why the teachers often are forced to construct a great part of the material themselves. Thus, the teaching process and the outcome of the teaching process can be explained in terms of organization of the contents, of the ability grouping of the pupils, and of the available time.

Recently a Swedish Government Official Report concerning the future curriculum was published. This report stresses the importance of freedom, individualization, and capacity to do independent work even more than the old curriculum. In this perspective Montessori teaching is not an old-fashioned method. For Montessori created a method which showed itself modern for the whole of the 20th century and much indicates that it is also a method which can face the demands of the next century!

Questions For Critical Reflection

1. What is the desirable balance among whole class, small group and individual activities?

2. Should the goal be to help the whole Grade 5 class achieve grade five levels of achievement by the end of the year, or to help each individual achieve personal levels within three or six year periods?

3. Is it reasonable to expect each teacher to create independently usable materials, or should teachers select the best textbooks available?

4. Is it reasonable to expect young children to accept responsibility, self-discipline, and self-motivation for independent study 70% of the time?

5. If whole-class teaching produces student passivity and conformity, won't many teachers value this for reducing discipline problems, making it the most practical way to teach?

FOOTNOTE
1. The description is an excerpt from my own lectures. Similar research results have been reported by Anderson & Burns, 1989; Cazden, 1986; Dunkin & Biddle, 1974.

References

Anderson, L. W. & Burns, R. B. (1989). *Research in classrooms: The study of teachers, teaching, and instruction.* Oxford: Pergamon Press (365 s).

Cazden, C. B. (1986). "Classroom discourse," in Wittrock, M.C. (Ed.). *Handbook of research on teaching* (Third edition). New York: Macmillan Publishing Company (s 432-463).

Dunkin, M. J. & Biddle, B. J. (1974). *The study of teaching.* New York: Holt, Rinehart and Winston, Inc.

Montessori, M. (1964). *The Montessori method* (first published in English in 1912). New York: Schocken Books.

Montessori, M. (1965). *Dr. Montessori's own handbook* (first published in English in 1914). New York: Schocken Books.

Montessori, M. (1973). *The Montessori elementary material.* Volume 2 of the Advanced Montessori Method (first published in English 1917). New York: Schocken Books.

Suggested Further Reading

Kramer, R. (1976). *Maria Montessori, a biography.* New York: G P Putnam's Sons.

Standing, E. M. (1957). *Maria Montessori: Her life and work.* New York: New American Library.

Chapter Nine

A Progressive School In Rockville, Maryland

Karen and Peter Day

History Of Progressive Schools

A brief look at the history of progressive schools demonstrates
an ongoing voice calling for child-centered classrooms in
which curiosity and inquiry are dominant factors as opposed to
a voice emphasizing such administrative and economic goals as
increased standardized test scores and centralized school systems. The aim of progressive educators has been that of helping
each child to fulfill his potential in informal settings. The aim
includes decentralized schools where decisions concerning the
goals and content of education are made by the teachers who
work with children affected by the decisions. This aim is in
dramatic contrast to that administrative initiative that moves to
centralized authority and increased formality.

The Progressive School movement began in the United
States in the 1840s. Horace Mann envisioned schools in which
children led a democratic life, developed strong character and
experienced growth through education in the arts. His vision
was thwarted by rapid growth among the newly established
public schools which brought with them increased numbers of
state run systems. In 1870 graded classes and graded texts

were introduced. The requirement to "cover" curriculum materials within a specified time led, for instance, to an overemphasis on children's memorizing of facts. While pedagogies were less concerned with the needs of the individual student, there was progress in that more students were educated. The concept of public school education for all children was being realized.

In 1879 Brooks Adams wrote an essay in the *Atlantic* that helped to turn educators back towards child-centered schools. He wrote, "Knowing that you cannot teach a child everything, it is best to teach a child how to learn" (Beringause, 1955).

At the end of the nineteenth century more voices were advocating a focus on fulfilling potential in children and on experiential learning rather than subject-based learning. Chief among these was Francis W. Parker, considered by many to be the father of the Progressive Education movement. When the rapid growth in the numbers of children to be educated gave rise to regimentation, Parker advocated flexibility. When states began to form state-wide requirements, Parker stressed the needs of the learner. When pedagogic practices stressed rote learning, Parker stressed exploration in learning. With this activist voice and educational philosophy, Parker became the first director of the University of Chicago School of Education.

A parallel movement in Chicago in the 1890s had a tremendous impact on progressive education. The Settlement House movement was led by Jane Addams and people who demanded increased numbers of elementary schools functioning in a child-centered environment. Among the movement's many goals was to increase the quality of community life through schools that emphasized a democratic, socially conscious leadership. For the first time both nursery and kindergarten programs were introduced into schools.

In the 1890s John Dewey became the voice and chief advocate for progressive education. He wrote about democratic living within the classroom and children learning by doing. Dewey, with his wife Alice, started the Laboratory School of the University of Chicago in 1896. This school still operates today, but was closed during the Depression. At this time Dewey went to Harvard and published a journal, *Progressive*

Education, which kept the ideals of the movement alive. Progressive schools continue today, but they enjoyed their greatest support in the 1960s.

What Is Progressive Education Today

Progressive education focuses on the individual child and the importance of constant questioning and reviewing of pedagogical practices by teachers. Every school with a "progressive" approach depends upon a philosophy and pedagogic practices that are formed by the people in that school. Clearly, each school is different, but progressive educators considered this unifying definition in 1983:

> A progressive school connotes an integration of disciplines, democratic ideals, participatory decision-making, focus on student education for a better world, education as a process rather than a product, helping individual needs. Progressive schools connote progressive attitudes: respect for children which allows them to learn in different ways in an atmosphere that gives them permission to explore and experiment. We need more than a limiting definition. We need to cultivate diversity (Jervis, 1983).

Ideals such as these provide guidance to those who struggle to both maintain consistency of quality education and to maintain the flexible attitude needed to bring out the best in teachers and students.

The following account of the events in a school year demonstrates the kind of learning and caring that took place in one progressive school. The recollections and reflections in italics are the experiences of a student who attended the school from 1975–1984 and in standard font by a teacher/parent who participated in the school community from 1975 to 1986.

Green Acres School

This nursery-to-grade eight progressive school is located in Rockville, Maryland, a suburb of Washington, D.C. In 1974–1984 there were three buildings, a lower school which housed nursery through grade six and the administrative offices, a smaller building for grades seven and eight, and a newly constructed gym/multipurpose building. The buildings were surrounded by a woods, a spacious playing field, sandboxes and playground equipment. Each room had a door to the outdoors which could be used as extended classroom space. It was also mundane, yet significant, that each room had its own toilet allowing children to leave the classroom when they felt the need and not be directed by adults.

Classrooms were generally clustered in groups of two grades, but this was a loose structure that saw walls put up and taken down as needs changed. The school opened its door to children in 1934 and continues to date with about 250 students and approximately 20 teachers. The average classroom size was 15 students which were combined and divided as curriculum and individual needs demanded. School began in early September.

September

School started with a very active week of outdoor education for students in grades five through eight. Teachers, parents and students organized an overnight trip to a camp along the Appalachian Trail. Duffel bags were packed with everything from sun-tan lotion to heavy socks and loaded onto the school bus with sleeping bags and snacks. Joe drove us to the wilderness camp in Virginia with a promise to return in three days.

The warm Septembers in this area allowed plenty of late summer canoeing trips, caving and rock climbing. I had a lot of experience canoeing, so I felt very confident in the stern. Caving was new to me, but I really enjoyed the cool damp cavern. This was not your normal tourist attraction, but a cave that you explored on your hands and knees, often slithering along on your stomach. At one point we turned off our lights and experienced the damp dark and silence. Later, it was very exciting to find salamanders and bats.

Rock climbing was a real challenge. I had no previous experience at this. Trained climbers tied me into a harness with the proper ropes. Two climbers "talked" me up the shear cliff. They told me to put my foot in one small space after another, places I felt were little more than a shadow. I fell once, but the ropes held and I again began the challenge of the rock. My group was cheering me on and I eventually made it to the top.

When we returned to the main camp there were group games. Jumping into a net held by other classmates was one we all did. The idea was to build trust among us. All the challenges were to build confidence in ourselves and to prove that we could overcome obstacles with the support of others. At the camp we could see that each of us had our strengths and weaknesses and that we could all succeed with each other's help. It was a lesson that was equally important here at the camp and in the classroom.

October

The primary unit, grades one and two, had sixty children and four teachers in a large open room. There was space for four individual groups, one in each corner, and an open centre area so we could gather all together. In October the centre area had a large wire cage which was home to Monarch butterflies. Students and teachers gathered milkweed leaves with tiny, golden eggs on the undersides and placed them in the wire enclosure. Soon black, green and yellow caterpillars hatched. They had to be fed many fresh milkweed leaves everyday because they grew very fast. Students gathered leaves at recess time. For 21 days we watched them grow. During this time students read books about butterflies like Jane Yolen's *Milkweed Days*. We read poems and wrote and illustrated logs about what we were seeing. The logs contained new words like "metamorphosis" and "chrysalis." Then we watched the caterpillar's body harden into a jade-coloured chrysalis. Each day we waited for the chrysalis to open. Finally, after three weeks, the small butterfly emerged and very quickly pumped-up its tightly packed wings to full size. The butterflies were fed sugar water for three days and then released. We would all gather outside and say good bye. We had plotted their long voyage to Mexico on a map, so we could think about where our butterflies would spend the winter.

November

Thanksgiving was a time for our entire community to celebrate. Two friends of the school came and prepared turkey dinner for the whole school. Each student also helped prepare for the celebration. Younger children coloured placemats and made table decorations. Older children set tables and grade seven students served everyone. Each table had a student from each grade, some of the kids were brothers and sisters of friends or kids you got to know on the bus. One grade eight student sat at each table to act in the "parent" role. Each year we did something different to prepare for the dinner. There were always stories told by teachers of favorite Thanksgivings and songs sung by all.

December

Before school had started in September, parents were invited to talk to teachers about their hopes and expectations for their children. Teachers thought of parents as their child's best advocate. It was a listening time for teachers. December was the time for the first formal report of the year in meetings between parents, students and teachers.

Early in the month we had a "Teacher's Tuesday". The children went home at noon, giving the teachers time for meeting. Each child had five or six teachers who all met to share ideas about the student's progress and to form a report. Teachers had a "report card" which gave structure to the items they discussed. Sitting around tables the teachers discussed a child's personal behaviour, sharing observations about the child's self control, response to guidance, her ability to follow through on commitments, and her ability to accept responsibility for her own action. Group behavior was also important. The teachers noted the child's ability to listen attentively, to contribute ideas in discussions, to consider others' ideas and feelings, to respect the rights of others to work undisturbed and to share the teacher's attention. A third area of observation concerned the child's work habits. It was important to the teachers that children were able to follow directions, organize their materials, put forth their best effort and seek help when needed. The teachers prepared samples of children's work to share with parents. The samples represented all areas of the curriculum: speaking, composition, reading, handwriting and spelling, math, social studies, art, music, science and physical education. Each "home-room" teacher had conferences with fifteen students and parents.

In addition to meeting with teams of teachers about each child, home-room teachers would hold conferences with individual students to talk about the same items that had been brought out by the teachers. Children were generally very candid about their ability to work both individually and in a group. It was important for each teacher to discuss with the child what she did best. It was a time of confirming strengths, as well as suggesting areas for growth. The conferences were scheduled for two days and evenings. The administrators worked very hard to schedule a time when all the adults who cared for a child could attend school with their students to share and celebrate their efforts and progress.

January

Each year the entire school studied one country. While there was collective agreement on the country to be studied, grade-level groups planned their objectives individually. The objectives included both satisfying individual interests of students and the growth of needed skills. The studies always ended in a whole school celebration of learning.

The goals of pursuing a study undertaken by the entire school were to build a sense of community, both within the school as children worked on a common theme and prepared for the celebration, and beyond the school to issues and understandings of the greater community. Parents and guest speakers were invited to share their interests and talents.

The selection of Japan one year serves as an example of the integrated curriculum emphasis of the school. We learned ethnic dances and sports in physical education classes and in music we sang Japanese children's songs and listened to a parent of Japanese birth play the koto. We each had a chance to play a short piece with the musician's encouragement. There were Japanese stories and poetry. Many groups wrote haiku for the school newspaper. Older students studied Japanese history and political issues to prepare for debates. And of course, each group had a chance to prepare some Japanese food to share at the celebration.

February

Green Acres was governed by a board of trustees that included parents, teachers, and administrators. In February the board and the staff met for a two and a half day retreat. It was a time of inquiry and community.

One year the first evening began with a dinner and a film, *Storm Boy*, that led to a discussion about what we thought learning was and how it felt when one learns. The next day began a discussion of the school's philosophy. Every two or three years, the staff would review the philosophy and question it. Areas of concern would centre around our philosophy of child development, questioning what we believed about how children grew and how they learned. We would be concerned about the kind of environment we wanted to foster as a learning environment and the kind of curriculum that we wanted to include. There were always discussions about the balance between flexibility of content and the need for children to learn skills. We talked about our value of stimulating new ideas and how to achieve that in the classrooms. A dialogue continued through the evening about our value of presenting plays. We asked how to balance the benefits for learning from these experiences with the time involved. We also spent time talking about how parents and teachers could build a stronger community that benefited every child. When we finished we wrote what we valued and printed it for our entire school community to read. These discussions and decisions guided our curriculum planning and our fiscal responsibilities for the rest of the year. The values that we teachers agreed upon reflected our best effort to make sense of our profession. The values afforded challenges for growth and a sense of community understanding.

March

Outdoor education and special events were very much valued in the progressive school community, but not more so than the value placed on the work done by students in the classroom. Units were formed of two grades in order to give teachers more flexibility in working with children on their instructional level. Such an arrangement necessitated tight scheduling, but teachers worked hard to preserve some flexible time as well. Mornings were more structured in order to allow for lessons in language arts and math. During this time children also met with art, music and science teachers. This arrangement allowed classes of approximately seven to ten students to receive direct instruction in language arts and math, while classes in art, music and science had 15 students.

Classes of seven to ten allowed teachers to individualize instruction. Many fiction and non-fiction trade books were used for reading instruction and teachers believed in the "write" way to read. In other words, reading and writing were taught as complementary processes. Often the selection of books depended on the theme that was being studied in social studies or science. It was in this context that words for spelling lists were chosen. In addition to a common spelling list, students also had individual lists that were generated from their individual reading.

The methods for teaching classes were varied. There were teacher directed classes, but more often students worked in groups or pairs on research questions. Grade 3 students researched animals of their choice, for example, and older students would research the background information needed for a debate. Class discussions stressed oral language and everyone was expected to participate. In small classes it was difficult to "hide in the corner.".

April

April always signaled the science initiated unit on birds for grade seven students. The unit culminated in a three day trip to the Chincoteague Wildlife Refuge for first-hand observation.

In science class we studied the birds' anatomy and bird families and acquired an ability to use Roger Tory Petersen's identification book in the field. Library classes were used both for research about birds and for reading stories such as *Snow Goose* by Paul Gallico (1941) and a chapter, "Voyage Eight: 1822," from Michener's (1978) book *Chesapeake* about Canada geese. In social studies, students plotted flight paths on maps and discussed conservation issues. Like so many studies at Green Acres, the theme was integrated to provide a context for learning. Underlying the theme was an awareness of the necessary skills needed for growth. Themes provided the motivation needed for learning to take place in a positive atmosphere.

May

The international Olympics Games are an event that take place once every four years, but the Green Acres' Olympics end every school year. Three teams, formed of students from grades six, seven and eight, played for team glory. The goal was to bring a positive ending to the school year and to introduce the grade six students to the team of teachers and to the students that they would be working with the following year.

In preparation, we made banners for the Corinthians, the Athenians and the Spartans, as well as gold, silver and bronze medals. (Everyone who played received a medal made of plaster and paint.) On warm afternoons before the games we acted Greek plays and read myths.

As soon as teams were formed of an equal number of students from each grade, we decided who would participate in which events. We wanted the best people in each event to gain the most team points. Some events included everyone, so physical education classes were used to coach the teams on better group game skills. Australian trollies had to be made from 2X4s and ropes, and then eight students had to figure out how to get coordinated enough to make them go quickly forward. Individual events included a bubble-gum blow, stare down and more demanding games like table-tennis, arm wrestling and races.

On the morning of the day that the games opened, the entire school met outside to take "our" Olympic oath in which we swore to play fairly, support our favorite team in a positive way and have fun. All of the younger kids were spectators and they usually cheered for their sister or brother's team. The days were hot so the first day ended with a gauntlet of water balloons to cool us off, and the second day ended with a water slide that we made from a plastic sheet. We also got a break from the hot sun at lunch-time when there were "brain brawls" and "name that tune" contests.

On the morning of the third day the scores were tallied and the entire school gathered for the medal awards and end-of-the year speeches. Then we celebrated with watermelon and said good-bye to friends.

Conclusion

In the introduction to this set of papers the patterns of teaching and learning that Goodlad saw as pervasive in the classrooms were discussed. By comparing Goodlad's patterns with those at Green Acres, the reader can recognize differences within some common areas.

Goodlad's first pattern was the dominance of whole-class teaching. At Green Acres School the class size was fifteen students, about half the number of students in many public schools. Therefore, a whole-class activity involved fewer students at Green Acres. Whole-class activities constituted one of the teaching patterns used by teachers, but during direct instruction in math or writing and reading for instance, the groups were small enough for individualized learning. Children often worked in pairs, perhaps reading to each other on the carpet or working on a poster. Classrooms had centers which encouraged individualized study and thereby allowed teachers to work with small groups. No one pattern was dominant and both furniture and space were flexible enough to suit a variety of patterns.

Second, Goodlad found competitiveness to be a dominant pattern among students. The emphasis at Green Acres was to encourage children to compete with themselves. Teachers said to students, "Last week you accomplished something. Can you better your record this time?" This value was visible in every area of the school from physical education classes to spelling records. All of the Green Acres' sports teams that played in city leagues with other schools included every student in the class and every student played. More able athletes were responsible for helping less able students to capitalize on their strengths.

At Green Acres the curriculum was planned by the teachers just as Goodlad observed. But often each student did not learn the same information. For example, the grade seven students studied birds as part of the science curriculum. Within that broad area of study the students made choices. The same was true of a social studies unit. Japan might be selected by the teacher, but the choice of individual reports was made by students. Students also selected the library books that they read. (Such curricula seldom employed a text book.) This allowed each student to read at a level that was comfortable for him, to participate in the overall study and to feel successful.

There was a mandate at Green Acres to help each student find his strengths and to use those strengths to accomplish those tasks that were more difficult for the student. This meant that the teachers had to be willing to allow students to complete tasks in a variety of ways. The result of a pedagogy that encouraged students to identify their strengths was to help students to control their mode of learning and to gain a sense of themselves. Praise for a job well done added up to an authentic sense of greater self confidence.

The variety of activities in the classroom was a boon both to the teacher and to the students. Experienced learning was a value that was proposed by John Dewey that provided meaningful lessons for Green Acres students. Green Acres had its own buses that took older students to bird sanctuaries, local historical sites or younger children to a corner store to practice counting change as a math exercise. Integrated curricula helped students to make meaningful connections and not feel fragmented. When children returned to the classroom they used both language and non-language skills to understand their experiences better. For instance, they would both write stories and develop photographs to capture their learning.

Children who had direct experiences as part of their learning and who had control over many of the processes of their learning were active and happy to be at school. Each day was not perfect for every child and teacher. On days when nothing seemed to go right there was experienced support to help and to remind us that each of us had strengths which could be used to get over the bumps in the road and that choices of alternative paths toward our teaching and learning goals could be made.

References

Beringause, Arthur (1955). *Brooks Adams: A biography*. New York: Knopf.

Gallico, P. (1941). *Snow Goose*. New York: A. A. Knopf.

Jervis, Kathe (Ed.) (1983). *Reunion, reaffirmation and resurgence: Notes and keynotes from the Miquon conference on progressive education.* Miquon, PA: The Miquon School.

Michener, J. (1978). *Chesapeake.* New York: Random House.

Epilogue

Alternative Schools As Critique Of Traditional Schooling

Chuck Chamberlin

Each of the alternative classrooms or schools described in the preceding chapters offers a critique of the traditional classroom described by John Goodlad and Larry Cuban in their extensive studies of classroom life and its effects. Both the traditional classrooms and the alternatives suggest certain ideals being passed on to the next generation. Some of these ideals can be identified as conceptions of the good person, the good citizen, and the good society. These ideas are often embedded in the hidden curriculum of classroom life, and are learned as students learn their approved norms and relationships with those in authority, and the values represented in those norms and in their textbooks and other curriculum materials. Analyses of the hidden curriculum have been written by Philip Jackson (1968), Michael Apple (1971), Henry Giroux and Anthony Penna (1979), Paulo Freire (1972), and Peter McLaren (1989) among others. The following descriptions of ideals implicit in the hidden curricula of traditional and alternative classrooms draw on those earlier analyses, and offer teachers choices among ideals, goals, and teaching philosophy. Cuban concluded that if change is to occur in classroom living, teachers need to reexamine and clarify their ideals. It is hoped that reflecting on the alternative ideals which follow will help teachers do that.

I

Traditional Classroom Ideals

The portrait of traditional classrooms painted by Goodlad and Cuban presents particular roles for teachers and for students, and consequent relationships between those with much authority and those with little. These roles and relationships result in students learning how to live and act in a community, and so suggest ideals of good person, good citizen, and good society. Goodlad found that whole class teaching was dominant, enabling the teacher to "maintain orderly relationships" (p. 123). The teacher was the central figure in determining classroom activities, maintaining virtual autonomy over decisions about materials used, classroom organization, instructional procedures, seating, grouping, content, use of space and time, and learning activities. During instruction, 75% of the talk was by teachers, mostly telling, with less than 1% "involving reasoning or perhaps an opinion from students" (p. 229). Student roles were mostly "listening or appearing to listen to the teacher and occasionally responding to the teacher's questions, ... working individually at their desks on reading or writing assignments ..." (p. 230).

Goodlad suggests the effect of these roles and relationships on students is that, "One learns passivity. Students in schools are socialized into it virtually from the beginning" (p. 233). The 13 years of experiencing teacher dominated classroom community life powerfully constrains growth in individual flexibility, originality, and creativity, and instead promotes contrasting characteristics: "... students experience school and classroom environments that condition them in precisely opposite behaviors — seeking 'right answers,' conforming, and reproducing the known" (p. 241). The dominance of the teacher limits student-initiated activity and leads to "quiet passivity" of students.

Good Person

Life in such classroom communities gets students used to expecting certain roles, certain relationships to those in authority, certain norms which become accepted ways of behaving, and certain values as guiding group behaviour. This hidden curriculum tends to socialize students into becoming certain kinds of good persons.

The testing and grading emphasis suggests people should be competitive for individual rewards rather than cooperative for the group's welfare. Passive acceptance of authority often seems to be expected of the good person. Conformity to the norms and roles expected by the authority seems more desirable than critical and creative thinking about their actions and beliefs. While Giroux's (1983) and Willis' (1977) work suggests some students will begin to resist this authority and its preferred norms and values, Goodlad's work indicates the good person is expected to be obedient, compliant, conforming, competitive, and passive.

Good Citizen

The ideal 'good citizen' suggested by the hidden curriculum of the traditional classroom is a poor fit to the democratic ideal, and better suits the type of citizen prepared for life in autocratic societies. Because life in this classroom community is so heavily dominated by the teacher, and because students are expected to accept the teacher's decisions and authority passively and uncritically, the good citizen traits being promoted seem likely to be the opposite of those needed in democratic communities: knowledge is accepted from teacher and text authority rather than being personally and tentatively constructed; decisions about community life are expected to be made by authorities and passively accepted by citizens rather than citizens exerting influence individually and through groups with shared beliefs and goals; an external locus of control is more likely than an internal locus of control and a weak sense of political efficacy is more probable than a strong one; laws are likely to be obeyed uncritically and public order prized over protest against injustice; and trust of those in power is more prized than skepticism. The 'ideal citizen' nurtured by the norms, relationships, values and hidden curriculum of the traditional classroom wouldn't seem to augur well for successful future democratic community life.

Good Society

The 'ideal society' promoted by living in traditional classrooms is suggested by the models of good person and good citizen outlined above. Such a society is described by Barber in his book *Strong Democracy* (1984) as 'thin democracy,' where 'thin' refers to the minimal role played by the citizenry in the governance of their communities — local, provincial, national and global. In such a society, the individualism and competitiveness learned in school and society lead most citizens to invest the least time feasible in community affairs, expecting elected officials and their appointed civil servants to provide good governance. However, as Newmann (1975) has pointed out, such 'thin democracy' often results in the continuing domination of a white, male, middle aged, upper-class, who take a conservative stand on social issues. The low sense of political efficacy and external locus of control nurtured in schools by roles of passivity and acceptance of authority likely contribute to a polarized society in which active citizenship and political influence are unequally distributed on class and race lines.

More recently, John Kenneth Galbraith (1992) has described this polarity in influencing governance as deeply embedded in our culture and its institutions, leaving the poor, the blacks, the underclass feeling helpless to exert influence, while the white, wealthy 'culture of contentment' dominates politically, socially, and economically. Newmann argues that this unequal influence and participation violates the democratic principle of consent of the governed, and "that education is, in part, responsible for its failure" (p. 46). Newmann calls on educators to provide all students with experiences in active citizenship in preparation for adult participation in community governance. As we have seen, some of the alternative classrooms provide such experiences.

II

Tvind School Ideals

In some ways, the Tvind schools resemble the traditional schools Goodlad described. The teachers use a textbook based academic program which leaves students with little voice in what and how to learn. Basic rules are set out by the school officials and must be followed. Teacher tastes in art to decorate student rooms and classrooms are imposed on students, and the same is true for the selection of music presented at public concerts. Students must do their share of cleaning, meal preparation, serving, and other chores. These aspects would suggest ideal persons, citizens and society similar to those described above.

However, in other crucial ways the Tvind schools are very different, and these differences make clear that their ideals sharply contrast to those of traditional schools.

Good Person

Confidence and self-esteem are qualities clearly valued by Tvind teachers. The participation in big projects is intended to prove to students that they have the ability to accomplish projects of significant importance for themselves and their group. Seeing such accomplishments as their windmill, indoor swimming pool, international trips and others is intended to develop confidence, pride, and self-esteem.

Solidarity is similarly valued, as these big projects as well as daily chores and presentations about trips are all done by class or school groups. Individualism is not encouraged in the major activities that give Tvind students identity, but rather a strong sense of group membership is promoted, and the confidence noted above is more in 'us' than in 'me.' Students learn the power and importance of the group's ability to achieve impressive feats rather than of the individual's potency.

The good person in the Tvind program also has a balance of academic and practical knowledge. Because of participating in so many construction, maintenance, cleaning, travelling, presenting, and food preparation activities, Tvind students learn many practical skills in organizing and doing projects related to daily living. These skills are seen as important preparation for adult life, and one of the advantages of living in a residential school for eleven months of the year.

Unlike all other programs, the Tvind schools promote positive attitudes to living in non-family groups. The teachers live in the residential schools, pool parts of their salaries to buy buses and school buildings, form work parties for major maintenance and construction projects, and thereby model for students an alternative social group to the nuclear family. Students are shown how this model works every day, and teachers intend that this modelling of sharing in larger group living will impact on student beliefs about how to live their lives.

Finally the Tvind view of the good person includes a sense of responsibility for third world people. By operating a school to train volunteers to help in third world countries, by involving all students in fund raising projects to support their development efforts, by including Third-World songs in their school songbooks, and by having the principal lead discussions about Third-World events, the Tvind program aims to develop an inclusive sense of community which is global in nature, and which requires action to help those in less developed countries.

In these ways, then, the Tvind schools are committed to developing an ideal good person considerably different from that reflected in the roles and relationships learned by students in traditional classrooms.

Good Citizen

As the above 'good person' traits suggest, the Tvind ideal of good citizen emphasizes community solidarity, and membership in a global community. These citizenship qualities contrast to the traditional classroom's emphasis on the individual, with minimum participation in or responsibility for broader communities' governance or welfare.

Additional experiences in roles of participating in responsible decision making for group welfare are built into the preparation for the long trips each class takes. Rather than the decisions being made by the teacher as is typical in traditional classrooms, all student citizens in their classroom community are given responsibility for preparing some portion of the trip, such as mapping, purchasing food, currency conversion, etc. Teachers may see mistakes being made, but often let students experience the consequences and find group solutions. In these ways experiences are planned to give all students opportunities to take responsibility for helping make decisions for group welfare, and do some of the work for group welfare. These roles and relationships to authority should promote an internal locus of control and perhaps some sense of political efficacy as students learn to participate in making group plans and decisions, and to carry them out.

While the elementary school children didn't appear to have any formal organization for school governance, the secondary students did have 45-minute daily meetings to discuss and resolve problems and to plan projects as well as two-hour meetings each Friday for committee work and reports. Experience in planning and advocating projects, persuading the other members, working within the school budget, doing the work to carry out projects — all provided experience in active citizenship roles which should develop strong feelings of group membership, internal locus of control, and sense of political efficacy. These, then, seem to be the traits of the Tvind ideal citizen.

Good Society

This secondary school experience in group problem solving, planning and advocating proposals, seeking consensus, and doing the work to carry out group decisions is consistent with Barber's (1984) conception of a strong democracy. This conception of good society emphasizes equality of opportunity to participate in the necessary community 'talking through' of problems. Everyone's ideas and points of view are given equal right of expression. Everyone has the right to disagree with proposals, to suggest amendments and changes, to attempt to persuade the community to accept their views. Barber argues that in a strong democracy, democratic talk is essential, "where no voice is privileged, no position advantaged, no authority other than the process itself acknowledged" (p. 183). This equality seemed to prevail in the Tvind meetings, casting students in roles and relationships to authority more consistent with democratic society than the teacher-dominant communities in traditional schools.

Other evidence of valuing an egalitarian society is found in the sharing of daily chores by all students in both elementary and secondary schools. Everyone takes a daily turn cleaning the toilets, washing the windows, vacuuming, washing and cleaning the buses, dusting, preparing and cleaning up after meals, and groundskeeping. The good society is demonstrated to be one where equality not only applies in governance but also in getting the work done which is essential to the welfare of the community.

While the traditional teacher-dominant student-passive roles are common in the academic program of the Tvind schools, the hidden curriculum's promotion of an autocratic, bipolar society noted earlier as the 'good society' of traditional schooling is counterbalanced at Tvind by the egalitarian teacher-student relationship in secondary school governance and in sharing equally in doing the community's chores. In these ways, the Tvind schools develop values, norms, roles, skills, self-concepts and expectations more consistent with an ideal of egalitarian democratic society.

III

Red Deer, Swedish And Freinet Schools Ideals

There are several similarities between the Tvind schools and the Red Deer, Swedish and Freinet programs. These similarities run through the ideals of good person, good citizen, and good society, and result from the common element of student participation in governance of their school and municipal communities.

Good Person

Like the Tvind schools, the Red Deer, Swedish and Freinet programs planned experiences in which students took responsibility for making decisions for some of their school activities. Red Deer students used learning centers at which there were multiple activities to choose from. They also worked in three groups to plan their presentations to city council on how to control mosquitoes, with either parent or teacher support.

Similarly, several teachers at the two schools in Uppsala, Sweden gave their students considerable responsibility for selecting projects, topics, pacing, and groups in their school activities.

And the Freinet schools used classroom Cooperatives to provide a forum in which students formulated an agenda, took turns in leadership roles, and made decisions about everyday classroom problems.

This shift of power from teacher to students changes the image of good person from one who expects external control over and direction for their activities to a person who expects to take independent or group responsibility for many of the decisions about their life activities: what to do, when, how, and with whom.

Good Citizen

Again, similarities to the Tvind Schools is apparent. Experiences in governance were intentionally planned for students in all three schools to help them grow to expect to actively participate in governing their class or school or city. Tvind, Swedish and Freinet students had formally organized processes for students to actively take part in classroom or school governance: setting out the agenda of problems to be discussed and resolved; providing leadership during the formal meetings; sharing equal opportunity to speak on the issues and promote their solutions; voting on issues; and carrying out the solutions decided on. Red Deer students followed similar procedures, but focused on a municipal issue and acted on their solutions by making presentations to city council to persuade council to adopt their preferred solutions.

These participatory experiences reflect the kind of good citizen qualities Reimer (1981) noted in his research on 'just schools' (see chapter 3). These include an increase in the taking of responsibility over the years of schooling, growth in moral judgment, and growth in student moral behavior. Additionally, Ehman's (1980) summary of research on political attitudes in students indicates growth in sense of political efficacy and internal locus of control when they have such direct participation in resolving issues and in governance. Hence, the ideal good citizens implicit in the Red Deer, Swedish and Freinet schools are confident in their ability to influence public issues, skillful in conducting and influencing group meetings, skillful in using media and persuasion to influence those in authority positions, and feel responsible for acting to benefit the welfare of all members of their communities.

Good Society

The experience of living together in a community where students must share in the responsibility of self-governance suggests an ideal society which is democratic in the sense intended by Barber (1992, 1984), Wood (1984), Pateman (1970, 1989), Osborne (1991, 1988) and Chamberlin (1983). This view of strong democracy rejects the view of a society where citizens elect representatives who then actively govern while the citizenry are largely passive, similar to the classroom relationships learned in the classrooms Goodlad described. Instead, life in the Red Deer, Swedish and Freinet classrooms suggests the good society is one similar to that described for the Tvind schools above where citizens play an active role in setting the agenda for political debate, inform themselves about the facts, points of view, and vested interests related to issues, organize to exert influence, ally themselves with groups sharing their goals, and help select and elect candidates sharing their views. The development of such a society is supported by schools that provide experience in self-governance to build the needed positive attitudes and expectations toward effective participation, and the skills needed to build the knowledge that gives such active participation credence.

It is the kind of democracy Newmann (1975) describes as providing for the *active* consent of the governed. He points out that there is a difference between having the ideal right to exert influence on public affairs (active consent) and the reality of how institutions, including schools, operate to either foster or prevent such participation. Newmann cites extensive evidence that current society does not achieve active consent because most people have learned passive relationships with those in authority, such as teachers. Newmann concludes that lived experiences in exerting influence on public affairs, as in the Red Deer classrooms, is needed to develop the democratic society in which the ideal of active consent is achieved.

Similarly, Angell (1991) has extensively reviewed the research on effects of classroom climate, and concludes that:

> ... classroom climate mediates democratic citizenship outcomes through: (a) peer interaction in cooperative activities, (b) free expression, (c) respect for diverse viewpoints, and (d) student participation in democratic deliberations and decision making. Empirical findings support a relationship between these conditions and the development of positive sociopolitical attitudes, higher levels of moral reasoning, prosocial behavior, and sense of community in elementary classrooms. ... it is argued that because the classroom is a vital organ of a democratic system, democratic climate in elementary classrooms may be a sine qua non for promoting the goals of democratic citizenship education. (p. 241)

Other examples of schools in which students are provided with experience in active citizenship may be found in Blom (1987) — Swedish schools; Chamberlin (1990) — Canadian schools; Conrad and Hedin (1982) — American schools; and Lewis (1991) — American schools.

These four schools, Tvind, Red Deer, Swedish, and Freinet then have developed experiences for their students which reflect an ideal society of active participation in strong democracy.

IV

Joanne Randall's Self-Evaluating Classroom Ideals

Joanne's philosophy and teaching placed great emphasis on involving parents and children in the evaluation of a binder of the child's work, and using that evaluation to have all three — parents, child and teacher-write goals to direct future activities of each. Joanne spoke of empowerment of her students as a major purpose of this sharing of responsibility and power, and it would seem to represent different ideals than those implicit in Goodlad's classrooms.

Good Person

Joanne clearly wanted her students to feel more control over their own lives in school. The evaluation conferences began with students taking their parents through a binder of their work to enable the children to explain their progress to their parents. This shift from teacher-only evaluation suggests children should share in assessing their growth, and the conference should end with the follow-up use of a form in which children use this self-evaluation to write down goals for themselves. These student roles suggest they are capable of sharing goal-setting with their teacher and parents. The good person seems to be one confident in making decisions about their own future, having reflected on past experience. As they set out projects for themselves, seek resources in their community, set up learning centres for their peers, and again evaluate their own growth, these children are developing self-concepts and confidence which should contribute to their becoming self-directed life-long learners. This stands in contrast to the dependent roles learned in Goodlad's teacher-centered classrooms, and offers quite a different ideal for personal growth.

Good Citizen and Good Society

Joanne often encouraged students to work on projects in groups, where a common interest was shared. The archaeological dig three boys undertook was one example given. Another was two girls who researched shampoos and set up a centre to share their findings. These projects enable groups to come to agreement on goals, tasks to be undertaken by each member, resources to be collected, and how to share their findings with others in their classroom community. In the process students learn to share responsibility with others in small group communities, similar to the Barber version of learning strong democracy in local contexts first, expecting that the roles and relationships learned will find later application in larger communities in which we feel membership. The Tvind and Swedish schools illustrate how they helped students feel membership in larger classroom and school communities and experience sharing in the governance of those groups. Perhaps this would be a logical next step for Joanne's students as they grow toward becoming citizens who actively participate in democratic societies.

V

A Piagetian School
And A Montessori School's Ideals

Both the Piagetian school in Spain and the Montessori school in Sweden placed heavy emphasis on teachers preparing a rich classroom environment in which students had a multitude of materials and activities from which to select. Students could work independently or in small groups for much of the day. This strategy changed the roles and relationships of students and teachers substantially, and created a classroom climate contrasting to Goodlad's traditional classroom communities with their dominant whole-class, teacher-directed pedagogy. Consequently, the hidden curriculum will be substantially different in its impact on student norms, self-concepts, values and expectations. These differences are reflected in the implicit ideals which follow.

Good Person

The emphasis placed on self-directed learning in classrooms rich in learning materials and activities suggests that an important quality of the good person for both the Piagetian and Montessori teachers is self-reliant independent learning and problem solving. Rather than encouraging dependence through teacher direction of whole-class activities where all students are expected to use the same materials at the same pace, these teachers expect their students to take responsibility for many of those decisions, and consequently grow in independence. Good persons, rather than looking for external direction from authority, grow to expect to depend on themselves for decisions in their own best interests, often working with classmates sharing their interests. This opportunity for small group work should also promote development of a second ideal trait, social skills in cooperation, sharing, leadership, compromise, etc.

A related ideal for the Piagetian teachers was that the concrete materials and independent activities should lead to development of sequentially more complex thinking. Hence, the good person should be capable of formal thought, recognizing complex relationships, able to restructure earlier organization of ideas which can be developed by transforming simpler ideas. They seek full development of the human potential for formal thinking as Piaget envisioned it.

The Good Citizen and Good Society

Unlike the Tvind, Red Deer, and Uppsala schools, the Piagetian and Montessori schools described do not report designing into their programs specific provisions for student self-governance. Consequently it is less clear what ideals of citizenship and society are reflected in their pedagogy. The Piagetian school did provide for small group projects where the group had to make decisions about what materials to use, how to share the work, how to make their final presentations, etc. This suggests good citizens who share responsibility for helping their community make decisions and complete tasks, and a society in which equality in influencing decisions is expected. While these components of strong democracy are similar to those ideals attributed to the Tvind, Red Deer, Freinet, and Uppsala classrooms, there is less explicit provision for nurturing these traits in the Piagetian and Montessori schools, where cognitive development has a much higher priority.

VI

Progressive School Ideals

Dr. Day began her chapter on Progressive schools with historical context, noting the roles of Horace Mann, Francis W. Parker, Jane Addams, and John Dewey. She referred to the goals of "democratic ideals, participatory decision-making, focus on student education for a better world, education as a process rather than a product, helping individual needs ... permission to explore and experiment...." She cited examples of some of those goals at Green Acres School to work toward the following ideals.

Good Person

The school year began with wilderness canoeing, caving and rock climbing with the goals being to "build trust among us," to "see that each of us had our strengths and weaknesses and that we could all succeed with each other's help," and "to build confidence in ourselves and to prove that we could overcome obstacles with the support of others." Again at Thanksgiving, groups made up of all grade levels sat together as "a time for our entire community to celebrate." Similarly whole school projects such as feeding the butterflies or studying Japan emphasized the individual's membership in the school community. Clearly ideal persons were ones who felt solidarity with their group, expected to accomplish goals as a group, studied more in groups than individually, and focused more on cooperation than on competition. The good person needed to trust others, work with others on common tasks, gain and give support to others in the school, and share in school-wide traditional celebrations. It seems the good person was intended to be a confident individual with a strong sense of membership in a local classroom community and a broader school-wide community.

Good Citizen and Good Society

Unlike the program in the Tvind, Red Deer, Swedish and Freinet schools, the Progressive school had no formal provision for student participation in either classroom or school governance. This left each teacher to make decisions about curriculum, rules, roles and norms in their classroom. It is difficult to infer what these decisions imply about the ideal good citizen, as was true also in the Piagetian and Montessori schools. However, the good person ideals described above clearly point to a particular vision of a preferred society. It is to be one with a strong sense of solidarity, where the individual is expected to feel responsible for the success of projects undertaken by groups or by the whole school community. While these projects were chosen by the teachers and students were expected to accept those decisions, the projects were structured in ways which made their success dependent on contributions by all students. The good society at Green Acres School would seem to be similar to an oligarchy in which members actively supported the authorities' decisions about what broad goals and activities should be sought, felt solidarity with others in engaging in those activities, and perhaps accepted responsibility for developing and carrying out plans for specific projects which contributed to the broad goals. Perhaps this leaves the good citizen to accept the decisions of the authorities about general goals and projects while sharing in the planning of smaller contributing projects.

VII

Waldorf School Ideals

Rudolf Steiner's anthroposophic philosophy remains the foundation of Waldorf schools, and embedded in it are conceptions of the good person. Steiner also evolved beliefs about pedagogy which set out preferred teacher and student roles which define classroom community in which certain roles, norms and values are learned by students. These set out implicit societal ideals, and insofar as they reflect individuals' relationships with authority, also imply traits of the ideal citizen.

Good Person

Arts and crafts play a more prominent role in the Waldorf schools than in traditional schools. More class time is invested in daily flute playing, water color painting, orchestra, choral music, dance, drama, ceramics, textiles, eurhythmics, woodworking and metalworking than is common elsewhere. "The ideal is a balance between concentrated thinking and creative expression" because the arts and crafts "offer students an opportunity to give physical expression to their feelings" and even have therapeutic value. The good person has developed a wide variety of forms of artistic expression to provide an outlet for their individual creativity and feelings.

The good person also values cooperation over competition. Competitive games are rejected, grading is replaced by written comments to reduce competitiveness, and it is desired that "the classroom environment should be permeated by a feeling of cooperation." Older students are expected to model this behavior for the younger children.

Waldorf teachers also hold other values concerning the good person, and "pupils cannot avoid being influenced by the values that pervade their education or adopting the attitudes the school attempts to inculcate in them." The schools oppose "competition, market-economic thinking, "consumer-society," etc."

Good Citizen and Good Society

The roles of teachers and students and the relationship of students to authority change from the lower grades to the upper grades. Teachers in the lower grades stay with the same group of students for seven years so that the teacher can "be like a parent, and during the first few school years should exert strong authority." This is consistent with the teacher-student relationship during teaching, where the teacher is to master rhetoric and "the conveying of information via the teacher is in fact an expression of his/her authority."

The roles, relationships and norms experienced by students in these early years is quite similar to what Goodlad and Cuban describe as common in traditional schools, and the implicit models of good citizen and good society are similar. In these classroom communities students appear to be learning passive, obedient acceptance of authority in a micro-society which is authoritarian in structure.

However, in the upper grades, students are to "eventually take responsibility for themselves and practice co-determination. Student democracy corresponding to that found in the Swedish public schools does not emerge until the seventh grade, after which point it becomes more and more pronounced." Apparently as students gain more maturity they are expected to co-plan with their teachers to an increasing degree, and a corresponding change in roles, relationships, norms and values makes up a contrasting hidden curriculum, more along the lines of the ideals noted earlier for the Swedish schools in Uppsala. The good citizen and the good society implied in this case would be more along the lines of active participation in an egalitarian democracy as advocated in Barber's *Strong Democracy*.

Conclusion

Cuban has been cited earlier as believing that traditional teacher-dominated classrooms have been so impervious to change because teachers have not developed strong personal belief systems and philosophies from which to evaluate such pedagogical traditions. This book has attempted to describe several alternative forms of classroom practice, and in this concluding chapter, to contrast the ideals implicit in those alternatives. It is proposed that ideals point to particular ways of teaching which prepare students to take particular citizenship roles in differing forms of society. Often the core of these differences revolve around competing conceptions of the desirable distribution of power among students/citizens and teachers/authorities. In the various classrooms and schools described here, the reader is presented with a range of choices of ideals and corresponding pedagogies. Hopefully, this epilogue will help make the hidden curriculum and implicit ideals less opaque, and will contribute to teachers developing personal ideals with which to evaluate alternative classroom practices.

In the process of thinking through these choices, teachers may need to ask:

- What traits do I believe characterize the good person?
- What classroom roles, relationships, norms and experiences will best nurture growth in those traits?
- What traits do I believe characterize the good citizen?
- What relationships to authority in my classroom will best nurture those traits?

- What kind of society is my ideal?
- What kind of classroom community living will best prepare students for that ideal society?

References

Angell, A. V. (1991). "Democratic climates in elementary classrooms: A review of theory and research," *Theory and Research in Social Education, 19*(3), 241–266.

Apple, M. (1971). "The hidden curriculum and the nature of conflict," *Interchange, 2*(4), 27–40.

Barber, B. (1984). *Strong democracy.* Berkeley, CA. : University of California Press.

Barber, B. (1992). *An aristocracy of everyone: The politics of education and the future of America.* New York: Ballentine Books.

Blom, M. (1987). *Citizenship education in Sweden.* A paper presented at the National Council for the Social Studies Annual Meeting, Dallas.

Chamberlin, C. R. (1983). "Knowledge + Action = Citizenship," in Parsons, J., Milburn, G., & Van Manen, M., (Eds.) *A Canadian social studies.* Edmonton: University of Alberta.

Conrad, D. & Hedin, D. (1982). *Youth participation and experiential education.* New York: Haworth Press.

Cuban, L. (1984). *How teachers taught: Constancy and change in American classrooms, 1890–980.* New York: Longman.

Ehman, L. (1980). "The American school in the political socialization process," *Review of Educational Research, 50*(1), 99–119.

Freire, P. (1972). *Pedagogy of the oppressed.* New York: Herder & Herder.

Galbraith, J. K. (1992). *The culture of contentment.* Boston: Houghton-Mifflin.

Giroux, H. (1983). *Theory and resistance in education: A pedagogy for the opposition.* South Hadley, MA. : Bergin & Garvey.

Giroux, H. & Penna, A. (1979). "Social education in the classroom: The dynamics of the hidden curriculum," *Theory and Research in Social Education, 7*(1), 24–48.

Goodlad, J. (1984). *A place called school.* New York: McGraw-Hill.

Jackson, P. (1968). *Life in classrooms.* New York: Holt, Rinehart & Winston.

Lewis, B. A. (1991). *The kid's guide to social action.* Minneapolis: Free Spirit Publishing.

McLaren, P. (1989). *Life in schools.* White Plains, N.Y.: Longman.

Newmann, F. (1975). *Education for citizen action*. Berkeley, CA. : McCutcheon.

Osborne, K. (1988). *Educating citizens: A democratic socialist agenda for Canadian education*. Toronto: Our Selves/Our Schools.

Osborne, K. (1991). *Teaching for democratic citizenship*. Toronto: Our Selves/Our Schools.

Pateman, C. (1970). *Participation and democratic theory*. Cambridge, U.K.: Cambridge University Press.

Pateman, C. (1989). "Feminism and democracy," in C. Pateman, *The disorder of women: Democracy, feminism and political theory*. Cambridge, U.K. : Polity Press.

Reimer, J. B. (1981). "Moral education: The just community approach," *Phi Delta Kappan, 62*(7), 485–487.

Willis, P. (1977). *Learning to labour: How working class kids get working class jobs*. Ferrborough, U.K.: Saxon House.

Wood, G. E. (1984). "Schooling in a democracy: Transformation or reproduction?" *Educational Theory, 34*(3), 219–239.

Join The Debate
On What Should Happen
In Canada's Schools.
You Can Still Get Your Own Copy
Of Each Of These Issues
Of Our Schools/Our Selves.

Issue #1: (Journal) A Feminist Agenda For Canadian Education ... The Saskatoon Native Survival School ... School Wars: B.C., Alberta, Manitoba ... Contracting Out At The Toronto Board ... On Strike: Toronto Teachers And Saskatoon Profs ... Labour's Message In Nova Scotia Schools And Ontario ... The Free Trade Ratchet ...

Issue #2: Educating Citizens: A Democratic Socialist Agenda For Canadian Education by Ken Osborne. A coherent curriculum policy focussed on "active citizenship." Osborne takes on the issues of a "working-class curriculum" and a national "core" curriculum: what should student's know about Canada and the world at large?

Issue #3: (Journal) B.C. Teachers, Solidarity and Vander Zalm ... The Anti-Streaming Battle In Ontario ... The Dangers of School-Based Budgeting ... "Whole Language" In Nova Scotia ... Vancouver's Elementary Schools 1920-60 ... The Maritimes in Song and Text ... Teaching "G-Level" Kids ... The Squeeze On Alberta's Teachers ... In Winnipeg: "The Green Slime Strikes Back!" ...

Issue #4: (Journal) Teaching The Real Stuff Of The World: Bears, History, Work Skills ... Tory Times At Sask Ed ... The NDP At The Toronto School Board ... Indian Control In Alberta Schools ... Is The Action Affirmative For Women School Board Workers ... Radwanski: The Dark Side ... More On "Whole Language" In Nova Scotia ... A Steelworker's Education ... B.C. Teachers Hang Tough ... Decoding Discrimination ...

Issue #5: Building A People's Curriculum: The Experience Of La maîtresse d'école edited with an introduction by David Clandfield. Since 1975 this Montreal teacher collective has been producing alternative francophone curricula on labour, human rights, peace, and geo-political issues in a framework of cooperative learning. This is an anthology of their best work.

Issue #6: (Journal) Labour Education And The Auto Workers ... Nova Scotia's Children Of The State ... Patrick Watson's *Democracy* ... Popular Roots Of The "New Literacy" ... Canada's Learner Centres ... Right-Wing Thinking In Education ... Fighting Sexism In Nfld. ... The Computer Bandwagon ... *Glasnost* and *Perestroika* Over Here? Funding Native Education ...

Issue #7: Claiming An Education: Feminism and Canadian Schools by Jane Gaskell, Arlene McLaren, Myra Novogrodsky. This book examines "equal opportunity," what students learn about women, what women learn about themselves and what has been accomplished by women who teach, as mothers and teachers.

Issue #8: It's Our Own Knowledge: Labour, Public Education & Skills Training by Julie Davis et al. The clearest expression yet of Labour's new educational agenda for the 1990s. It begins with working-class experience in the schools and community colleges, takes issue with corporate initiatives in skills training, and proposes a program "for workers, not for bosses."

Issue #9: (Journal) Rekindling Literacy In Mozambique ... Privatizing The Community Colleges ... CUPE's Educational Agenda ... High Schools & Teenage Sex ... Workers And The Rise Of Mass Schooling ... More On Nova Scotia's Children Of The State ... Grade 1 Learning ... Private School Funding ... The Globe's Attack on Media Studies ... "Consolidation" in P.E.I. ... Manitoba's High School Review ...

Issue #10: Heritage Languages: The Development And Denial Of Canada's Linguistic Resources by Jim Cummins and Marcel Danesi. This book opens up the issue of teaching heritage languages in our schools to a broad audience. It provides the historical context, analyzes opposing positions, examines the rationale and research support for heritage language promotion, and looks at the future of multiculturalism and multilingualism in Canada.

Issue #11: (Journal) No More War Toys: The Quebec

Campaign ... Labelling The Under-Fives ... Building A
Socialist Curriculum ... High School Streaming in Ontario
... Growing Up Male In Nova Scotia ... New Left Academics
... Tory Cutbacks In Alberta ... More On Workers And The
Rise Of Mass Schooling ... The Elementary School Ruby
And How High School Turned Her Sour ...

**Double Issue #12-13: What Our High Schools
Could Be: A Teacher's Reflections From The 60s
To The 90s** by Bob Davis. The author leads us where his
experience has led him — as a teacher in a treatment
centre for disturbed children, in an alternative community
school, in a graduate education faculty, and for 23 years in
two Metro Toronto high schools. The book ranges from
powerful description to sharp analysis — from sex
education to student streaming to the new skills mania.

Issue #14: (Journal) Feminism, Schools And The Union
... What's Happening in China's Schools ... N.B. Teacher
Aides And The Struggle for Standards ... Barbie Dolls And
Unicef ... Post-secondary Cuts In Alberta ... CUPE-Teacher
Links ... Language Control In Nova Scotia ... Pay Equity For
Ontario Teachers ... Women's Struggles/Men's
Responsibility ...

**Issue #15: Cooperative Learning And Social
Change: Selected Writings Of Célestin Freinet**
edited and translated by David Clandfield and John Sivell.
Célestin Freinet (1896-1966) pioneered an international
movement for radical educational reform through
cooperative learning. His pedagogy is as fresh and relevant
today as it was in his own time, whether dealing with the
importance of creative and useful work for children or
linking schooling and community with wider issues of
social justice and political action. This translation is the
first to bring a broad selection of Freinet's work to an
English-speaking audience.

Issue #16: (Journal) B.C.'s Privatization Of
Apprenticeship ... Marketing Adult Ed In Saskatchewan ...
The Future Of Ontario's CAATs ... Edmonton's Catalyst
Theatre ... The Money Crisis In Nova Scotia Schools ... The
Politics Of Children's Literature ... Tough Kids Out Of
Control ... A Literacy Policy For Newfoundland? ... Métis
Schooldays ... Capitalism And Donald Duck ... In Struggle:

Ontario Elementary Teachers ...

Issue #17: (Journal) Towards An Anti-Racist Curriculum ... Discovering Columbus ... The Baffin Writers' Project ... The Anti-Apartheid Struggle In South Africa's Schools ... What People Think About Schooling ... Children's Work ... Radical Literacy ... Getting The Gulf Into The Classroom ... Bye-Bye Minimum C Grades ... Taking Action On AIDS ...

Issue #18: (Journal) Can The NDP Make A Difference? ... Columbus In Children's Literature ... Labour Takes On Ontario's Education Bureaucrats ... Lessons From Yukon Schools ... Vision 2000 Revisited ... Getting A Feminist Education The Hard Way ... Children In Poverty ... Reflections Of A Lesbian Teacher ... Literacy, Politics and Religion In Newfoundland ... Critiquing The National Indicators ... Student Loans In Saskatchewan ...

Double Issue #19-20: Teaching For Democratic Citizenship by Ken Osborne. In this book Osborne extends his work in *Educating Citizens* and takes us through the world of modern pedagogies and the most recent research on effective teaching. He focuses particularly on "discovery learning," "critical pedagogy," and "feminist pedagogy" — drawing from a wide range of classroom practice — and builds on this foundation the key elements of an approach to teaching in which democratic citizenship is the core of student experience.

Issue #21: (Journal) The Tory Agenda ... Higher Education For Sale ... Racism and Education: Fighting Back In Nova Scotia, In A Scarborough Collegiate, In South Africa And In Victoria's Chinese Student Strike ... Saskatchewan's Neo-Conservatives ... As Neutral As My Teacher, Jesus ... "Make Work" in New Brunswick ... Teachers Politics: In Ontario And Mexico ... A Feminist Presence ... Canada's Heritage Language Programs.

Issue #22: Their Rightful Place: An Essay On Children, Families and Childcare in Canada by Loren Lind and Susan Prentice. The authors examine the complex ways we view our children in both private and public life and the care we give them inside our families and within a network of private and public childcare. They also offer an historical perspective on families and childcare in Canada and propose a strategy to develop "a free, universally accessible, publicly-funded, non-compulsory, high quality, non-profit, community-based childcare system" right across the country.

Issue #23: (Journal) Corporate Visions ... Taking On The Montreal School Commission ... Postmodern Literacy ... A Neo-Conservative Agenda In Manitoba ... Facing Up To High School Sexism ... Education In The Age Of Ecology ... An Autoworkers' Education Agenda ... Learning About Work ... The Politics Of Literacy.

Issue #24: Stacking The Deck: The Streaming Of Working Class Kids In Ontario Schools by Bruce Curtis, D.W. Livingstone & Harry Smaller. This book examines the history and structure of class bias in Ontario education. It looks at both elementary and secondary schooling and proposes a new deal for working class children. The evidence is taken from the Ontario system, but the ideas and analysis can be extended to every school in Canada.

Issue #25: (Journal) The Meaning Of Yonge Street ... What Should The NDP Do? ... New Brunswick's Plunge Into 'Excellence' ... Bargaining For Childcare ... Denmark's Efterskoles ... Reader Response And Postmodern Literacy ... Against Skills ... Slash And Burn In Nova Scotia Schools.

Issue #26: Training For What? Labour Perspectives On Job Training by Nancy Jackson et al. In this book a number of union activists analyze the corporate training agenda in Canada and open up a labour alternative. They let us see training as a tool of political struggle in the workplace, which can contribute to skill recognition, to safe and satisfying working conditions, to career progression and to building a more democratic vision of working life.

Issue #27: (Journal) NAFTA's Destruction Of Canadian Education ... The Corporate Hijacking Of Canada's Universities .... Lining Up Gender In Elementary School ... Totems and Taboos In Bilingual Education ... Teaching Outside The Mainstream ... The Nuclear Agenda In Saskatchewan's Schools ... The Anti-Racist Uses Of To Kill A Mockingbird ... New Brunswick Reading Circles ... John

Dewey And American Democracy ... Surveying Canada's Teens ... Educating For Change.

Issue #28: Schools And Social Justice by R.W. Connell. Throughout this broad analysis, which spans the educational systems of Europe, North America and Australia, Connell argues that the issue of social justice is fundamental to what good education is about. If the school system deals unjustly with some of its pupils, the quality of education for all of the others is degraded. He calls for "curricular justice," which opens out the perspective of the least advantaged, roots itself in a democratic context, and moves toward the creation of a more equalitarian society.

Issue #29: (Journal) Teaching Mi'kmaq: Living A Language ... TV And The Dene ... Turning A Blind Eye To Linguistic Genocide ... After 1492–1992: A Post-Colonial Supplement For The Canadian Curriculum ... The Emerging Corporate Agenda For Canadian High Schools ... A Critical Look At The Skills Mania ... Show Boat: Reflections On The Passage Of A Racist Icon ... The Ninth OISE Survey: The Public Mood In Tough Times ... A New Vision For Bilingual Education.

Issue #30: Pandora's Box: Corporate Power, Free Trade and Canadian Education by John Calvert and Larry Kuehn. The authors lay bare the real story behind corporate interest in education and show, via a detailed analysis of the NAFTA text and political and economic trends throughout North America, how NAFTA is being used by Corporate Canada in their attempts to commercialize and privatize public education.

Issue #31: (Journal) The NDP and Education: What Happened In Ontario, B.C., Saskatchewan, and Manitoba? ... N.B.'s Strategy For Post-Secondary Education ... Gender Equity: A Personal Journey ... American Racism, Canadian Surrender: More Reflections On "To Kill A Mockingbird" ... A Letter From Siberia ... All The News That's Fit For Business: YNN Zeroes In On The Canadian Classroom ... Speak It! From The Heart Of Black Nova Scotia ... Educating The English.

Issue #32: Rethinking Vocationalism edited by Rebecca Priegert Coulter and Ivor Goodson. Returns us to some of the "old questions" about education — who controls it?, and whose interests are served by it?— as they examine the "reconfiguration" of vocational education in a period of global restructuring. Other authors include Christopher J. Anstead, Jean Barman, Catherine Casey, Kari Dehli, Jane Gaskell, Madeleine R. Grumet, Nancy Jackson, Jeffry Piker and Jim Turk.

Issue #33: (Journal) "Children Are Not Meant To Be Studied ..." ... Curriculum And Teaching In Canada: The Missing Centre ... More Training For What? The Canadian Labour Force Development Strategy, Saskatchewan Style ... The Regime Of Technology In Education ... Teacher Unions And Social Responsibility ... You Might Enjoy The Humble Pie At Pete's, Mr Coren ... Like Small Streams That Feed The Mississippi: Resistance In America Education ... The Lament Of A Passer-by ... Lies, Dammed Lies, And Statistics: Drop-outs, Literacy & Tests ... Education Roundup ... To Stream Or Not To Stream In Manitoba ... Getting Off The Track: Classroom Examples For An Anti-tracking Pedagogy ... Speaking Of Our World.

Subscribe Now!

In One Year You'll Receive 3 Journals And 3 Books.

It's Not Only A Great Read, It's A Great Deal.

Here's What's Coming In Future Issues Of Our Schools/Our Selves

---

Articles On:

Bombers, Kids, And Kites — Labour Studies At The Toronto Board — What Do We Tell Our Kids About Canada — "Gifted" Education — Science And Standardized Testing — Public Education In The Globe and Mail — Environmental Activism — Unionizing ESL Teachers — A Winnipeg Inner City School — CUPE's Fight For Parental Leave — The World Of Teenage Girls — The BC School Wars Continue — Labour, Education And The Arts — Sex In Upper Canada's Classrooms — Young Women In Trades — Education Politics In Alberta — Inside The Labelling Process — Schools And Museums — Whatever Happened To York University?

You'll get three journals and three books a year for each subscription.

Books On:

Sex in School — Teaching History — A Socialist-Feminist Approach To Phys Ed — Native Control Of White Education — Whatever Happened To High School History? — Assessment And Evaluation — Australian Education Activism — What's Basic? A Teachers' Union Response To Bob Rae's Assault On Ontario Schools — Racism and Education — Where Is The US Left In Education? — What Do People Really Think About Our Schools? — An Anti-Racist Curriculum For Nova Scotia — The Canadian Intellectual Tradition — A People's History of Canada

---

It's a great bargain, as much as 50% off the newstand price.

Subscribe Today

OUR SCHOOLS / OUR SELVES

Bringing together education activists in our schools, our communities and our unions...*with your help* !

Please enter my subscription for 6 issues of OUR SCHOOLS/OUR SELVES starting with issue number_____. Please check one:

INDIVIDUAL
_____ Regular rate $34.00
_____ Student/Unemployed/
     Pensioner rate $28.00
_____ Outside Canada   Cdn $46.00

ORGANIZATION
_____ In Canada $50.00
_____ Outside Canada   Cdn $60.00
SUSTAINING
_____ $100   _____ $200   Other $_____

OR send me issue number(s) _____ at $9.00 per single and $16.00 per double issue

Name_____

Address_____

City_____ Prov_____Code_____

Occupation_____

___ Cheque enclosed   ___ Bill me later   ___VISA / Mastercard

Card No_____Expiry date _____

Signature_____

Pass to a friend

OUR SCHOOLS / OUR SELVES

Bringing together education activists in our schools, our communities and our unions...*with your help* !

Please enter my subscription for 6 issues of OUR SCHOOLS/OUR SELVES starting with issue number_____. Please check one:

INDIVIDUAL
_____ Regular rate $34.00
_____ Student/Unemployed/
     Pensioner rate $28.00
_____ Outside Canada   Cdn $46.00

ORGANIZATION
_____ In Canada $50.00
_____ Outside Canada   Cdn $60.00
SUSTAINING
_____ $100   _____ $200   Other $_____

OR send me issue number(s) _____ at $9.00 per single and $16.00 per double issue

Name_____

Address_____

City_____ Prov_____Code_____

Occupation_____

___ Cheque enclosed   ___ Bill me later   ___VISA / Mastercard

Card No_____Expiry date _____

Signature_____

**Business
Reply Mail**

No postage stamp
necessary if mailed
in Canada.

Postage will be paid by

OUR SCHOOLS/OUR SELVES
1698 Gerrard Street East,
Toronto, Ontario, CANADA
M4L 9Z9